Growing Vegetables and Fruit

Growing Vegetables and Fruit

BY ARTHUR BILLITT

Boots
BOOKS

Acknowledgements

Photographs
A-Z Collection, 89
Pat Brindley, 34, 54, 63, 65 (bottom), 95, 97, 105 (inset), 118
Valerie Finnis, 89 (inset), 96
Brian Furner, 18, 39 (inset top), 67, 105, 118 (inset)
The Hamlyn Group, 21, 25
The Harry Smith Horticultural Photographic Collection, 39 (inset bottom),
    51, 55, 56, 65 (top), 109 (inset), 115
Michael Warren, 26, 39, 62, 112, 119
Paul Williams, 10–11, 19, 22–23, 58–59, 68–69, 72–73, 80–81, 84–85, 100–101

Line drawings
Laura Mason 37, 40, 67, 107 (top), 117 (right)
All others by Angela Lewer

Endpapers show a range of gardening equipment available from
larger branches of Boots

Published for The Boots Company Limited by
The Hamlyn Publishing Group Limited
London · New York · Sydney · Toronto
Astronaut House, Feltham, Middlesex, England
© Copyright The Hamlyn Publishing Group Limited 1980

ISBN 0 600 391 744

Phototypeset in England by Tradespools Limited, Frome, Somerset in
11 on 12pt. Sabon
Printed and bound in Spain by Graficromo, S. A. – Córdoba

Contents

VEGETABLES

A well cared for vegetable-growing area can be just as attractive, although maybe not as colourful, as an ornamental garden. Certainly the rewards are very different. A vegetable garden usually provides a challenge not only to just grow vegetables well, but also to provide the family with fresher and better produce than can be purchased in the shops. The home gardener is able to concentrate on growing vegetables for quality, and particularly flavour. Unlike the commercial grower one has no need to consider such factors as resistance to damage in transit, shelf life and eye appeal.

When drawing up the balance sheet, providing the varieties have been carefully chosen for quality and flavour, the home gardener will always be in credit. The exercise involved in vegetable growing is healthy and the freshness of the produce ensures that the vitamins and minerals are still present when either the vegetables or the salads are presented at the table. It is impossible to put a price on the best quality and finest-flavoured garden vegetables as they are no longer available in the commercial market. Therefore growing them at home is the only answer.

The plot

The old idea of relegating the vegetable area to an out-of-the-way spot, often shaded by trees, is wrong. A full-sun position is best, excessive shade from trees or buildings results in plants with weak, drawn growth and poor cropping potential. Ideally the size of the vegetable garden should be related to the needs of the kitchen. At one time a 270 sq m (300 sq yd) allotment plot was considered about the right size for an average family; but in these days with gardens continuing to decrease in size, the area may have to be much smaller. For three years I have cultivated a plot measuring 6m by 3m (20ft by 10ft), which is only 18 sq m (200 sq ft), at Clack's Farm with results that have surprised me. I am sure it is just a question of planning if you wish to have fresh vegetables all the year round from your own garden.

Preparing the ground

Preparing a vegetable plot will depend on the

site. I have never been afraid of weeds, even the strong-growing perennials such as nettles, thistles, docks and couch grass being present do not deter me. I know that if the land is well dug before Christmas, with the grass and the weeds tucked underneath, surface cultivations will eradicate them during the first season. In years past I have gone to the trouble of trying to pick all the roots out but, however well I thought the job had been done, there were always too many left for the ground to be considered clean. No weeds, however tough, can survive a whole season if constantly denied the opportunity of making above-ground growth. To do this job thoroughly, a weekly, or even twice weekly, round with the Dutch hoe may be necessary in the first season.

Winter digging carried out before Christmas with the clods left unbroken, allows the frost to make its contribution; even heavy clay responds well to weathering. The golden rules for all soils, but particularly for heavy soils, are: dig and leave rough in the winter, make your seed and planting beds in the spring first with a three-pronged cultivator and then with a rake and never turn a heavy soil over with a fork or spade in the spring. Breaking these rules will result in unmanageable clods and loss of soil moisture, which means poor results.

Soil fertility

Starting with new ground usually means that the fertility level is reasonable. The grass and weed roots provide the fibre to keep the soil open and plant residues in various stages of decomposition supply nutrients. So without additions, except maybe garden lime for the brassicas if the soil is inclined to be acid, first-year results can be very good. However, without taking steps to maintain soil fertility, cropping results are bound to decline in succeeding years.

In nature plants return their foliage to the soil, animals and birds make their contributions: nothing is taken away that is not returned, so the fertility level remains fairly static. In vegetable growing goodness is taken away and it is up to the gardener to make good the deficiencies. This can be done by composting every scrap of waste vegetation: lawn mowings, leaves, peelings, vegetable tops and so on. However, prepared-food waste should not be added as this attracts vermin such as rats.

The compost heap

I build compost up in heaps, bins or in wire-netting circles placed on the soil surface. I employ a sandwich technique starting with 15-cm (6-in) layer of vegetable waste, treated alternately with a sprinkling of soil and garden lime. With the first 15-cm (6-in) layer of vegetable waste lightly trodden down I sprinkle a handful or two of garden soil over it, this supplies the soil bacterias which multiply and gradually get to work in the

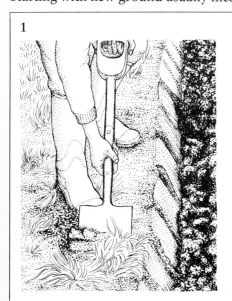

Digging

1 Take out a trench one spade blade deep. Skim off the weeds from the adjacent soil surface and place them in the bottom of the trench together with any other organic matter you wish to incorporate

2 When taking out subsequent trenches, throw the soil forward, inverting the spadeful on top of the organic matter

Compost containers

1 A simple circle of chicken wire or plastic netting supported by wooden stakes makes an easy-to-construct container

2 A heap can be supported on three sides by sheets of corrugated iron or other suitable material

3 A rather more sophisticated wooden bin with slatted sides which allows air to penetrate

1

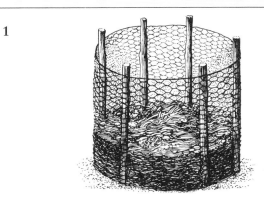

2

3

breakdown processes. When the next 15-cm (6-in) layer is complete and lightly compacted I sprinkle a handful of garden lime over it. this keeps the heap sweet and safe from becoming a soggy mess. This build up is repeated layer by layer until it fills the container.

In practice I find that it takes roughly six months before the compost is friable and ready for use, this means that the material at the bottom of the heap is ready first. With two compost heaps or bins in operation the top partially-decomposed waste of one can be used with advantage to make the start of another. An earth base is an advantage as the worms then lend their help to the process. Wooden bins should be slatted to allow aeration at the sides. If you have pre-fabricated plastic bins make sure these too have sufficient air holes. The incorporation of well-rotted compost during the winter digging helps to maintain fertility and reduces the risk of such problems as potato eelworm by providing food for the predacious fungi which trap and live on the potato eelworm.

Fertilisers

Crop yields can be increased considerably by the use of fertilisers; those formulated from organic ingredients are often preferred. So-called balanced fertilisers supply three essential plant foods; nitrogen, which encourages growth and plays a great part in leaf colour; phosphates, which are essential for root, flower and fruit development and potash, which is necessary for the maintainance of plant health and flavour and sweetness in the crop.

In addition to these three major elements calcium is also needed, for without it, it is impossible to get the full benefit of any fertiliser treatment. Garden lime used with discretion supplies calcium and at the same time reduces soil acidity. However, excessive use of garden lime induces trace-element deficiencies particularly those of iron, manganese and boron. Adequate amounts of most trace elements are usually present in garden soils, but trouble occurs when their uptake is interfered with by the use of other

13

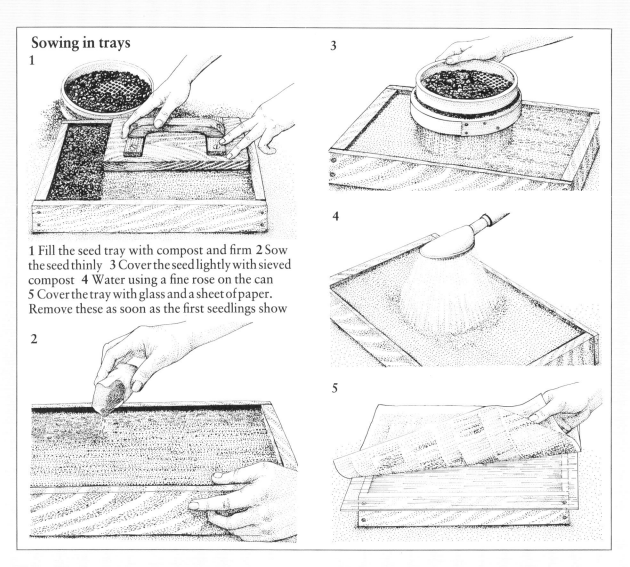

Sowing in trays

1 Fill the seed tray with compost and firm 2 Sow the seed thinly 3 Cover the seed lightly with sieved compost 4 Water using a fine rose on the can 5 Cover the tray with glass and a sheet of paper. Remove these as soon as the first seedlings show

elements. Many fertiliser formulations include trace elements as well as the three major elements.

Never apply garden lime at the same time as compost or manure as nitrogen will be liberated into the air and therefore lost to future crops. Incorporate manure and compost during the pre-Christmas digging and sprinkle on garden lime in the spring before sowing to get the maximum benefit of both soil improvers. Never apply garden lime on land where potatoes are going to be planted.

Crop rotation
However small or large the vegetable garden, the cropping should be planned on at least a three-year basis so that with the possible exception of runner beans, no crop is grown on the same spot more frequently than once in three years. Failure to adhere to a plan for crop rotation can result in serious pest or disease problems. It is relatively simple to divide the major crops roughly into three groups: brassicas (the cabbage family), legumes (peas and beans) and rootcrops including potatoes. Within this, intercropping can be carried out where possible with quick-maturing crops such as lettuce and radishes. Runner beans on account of their height are best sited at the north end of the plot to avoid shading other crops.

The seed bed
Preparation of a good seed bed is easy when the soil has been weathered after winter digging. However, do not start until the soil begins to dry out as walking on a wet, cold

soil will destroy its structure. A garden rake is the best tool for getting a good seed-bed tilth. It may be necessary to do the job in stages but even the heaviest soils respond to treatment.

For good germination of small seeds quite a fine tilth is needed and the seed should be sown fairly shallowly, some seeds only need a very slight covering of soil. It is a mistake to start outdoor sowing before the soil is ready or too early in the season. Observe the good gardening rules: sow when the soil is dry and plant when the soil is wet.

If possible raise your own brassica plants, the timely application of appropriate insecticides and fungicides can prevent most vegetable troubles but club root of brassicas and potato eelworm are still exceptions. Club root is usually brought into the garden by plants grown in infected soil, so do take care not to introduce any into your garden.

Tools

When buying tools it is wise to start with those that are essential, such as a spade, a fork, a hoe, a cultivator and a garden line (you can make this yourself out of two sturdy stakes and some strong twine at least the length of your longest cropping row). Never buy a spade or fork which is too heavy or too

Sowing outdoors

1 Draw out a drill using the corner of a rake held against a garden line
2 Sow seed thinly in the drill
3 Cover with soil and firm with the flat of the rake head

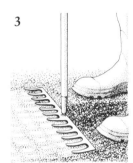

large for you. I prefer mine to have wooden shafts and my spade to have a thin blade; a heavy stainless-steel spade may look good but can be exhausting to use.

Crop rotation plan			
Year	**Brassicas**	**Legumes**	**Roots**
1	apply: sprinkling of lime in winter and a general fertilizer	apply: well-rotted compost or manure in winter	apply: a general fertilizer *Potato plot only* well-rotted compost or manure in winter
Year	**Legumes**	**Roots**	**Brassicas**
2	apply: well-rotted compost or manure in winter	apply: a general fertilizer *Potato plot only* well-rotted compost or manure in winter	apply: sprinkling of lime in winter and a general fertilizer
Year	**Roots**	**Brassicas**	**Legumes**
3	apply: a general fertilizer *Potato plot only* well-rotted compost or manure in winter	apply: sprinkling of lime in winter and a feneral fertilizer	apply: well-rotted compost or manure in winter

SALADS

It is probably in the area of salad crops that the advantages of home-grown produce are most apparent. Even in the tiniest of spaces, from a windowbox upwards, something can be grown to relieve the boredom of tired green salads and the tedium of those varieties which have been chosen only for their travelling ability and tolerance of shop life. With a sizeable growing area it is quite simple to lengthen the freshly-picked salad season, extending it well into the period from November to March when shop prices can be so high. By using glass for protected growing, the possibilities are there for all-the-year-round self-sufficiency in salads.

Chicory

Correctly grown the creamy-white heads, or chicons, provide salads throughout the winter and up to the end of March. To be palatable nearly all chicory should be blanched; any recommended as satisfactory without blanching have so far been too bitter for me. Chicory is easy to grow in a sunny open position, and providing they are well prepared, most soils are suitable.

Preparing the soil
It grows best on a site which has been manured for a previous crop. Do not incorporate compost or manure into the soil immediately before growing as a high level of organic material leads to the growth of forked roots which are less suitable for forcing. Deep digging in the autumn is advisable so that the long parsnip-like roots can easily grow downwards. Two weeks or so before sowing rake the seed-bed to a fine tilth and work in 30g of Growmore fertiliser per sq m (1oz per sq yd).

Sowing and cultivation
Sow in May in rows 30cm (1ft) apart. As soon

Forcing chicory
1 Lift roots in November. 2 Trim off the tops and shorten roots. 3 Put five roots in a pot and cover to exclude light.
4 Chicons will be ready in about five weeks.

as the seedlings are large enough thin to 25cm (9in) apart. Hoe regularly throughout the growing season to keep the rows weed free.

In October the leaves will begin to die down; when they are almost dead it is time to lift the roots for storing until they are needed for forcing. I am always careful to lift the full length of the root right down to the tip; pieces left behind are virtually root cuttings and liable to become a nuisance the next season.

To prepare the roots for storing, clean away all the dead foliage cutting straight across the leaf stalks well above the root crown, leaving a promising area for regrowth. Shorten the roots to 23cm (9in) and remove any side shoots. Pack them flat in boxes of dry sand and store where it is cool but frost free.

Sowing and Harvesting Chart

Crop	When to sow in the open	When to sow under glass	When to plant out	Distance between plants	Distance between rows	When to harvest
Chicory	May - July			23cm (9in)		November - March
Endive	April - July			30cm (12in)	38cm (15in)	August - February
Mustard and Cress		All the year round				3 weeks after sowing
Radish	March - July	February			15cm (6in)	approx. 4 weeks after sowing
Cucumbers winter	August			8cm (3in)	30cm (12in)	October - November
frame		March - April	April - May			June - September
ridge	May - June	April	May	60cm (2ft)	1m (3ft)	July - September
Lettuce	March - September	September - March	March	15-30cm (6-12in)	30cm (12in)	All the year round according to variety
Tomatoes		February - April	May - June	45cm (18in)	60cm (2ft)	May - October

Forcing

Forcing can be carried out from December to March. By setting up a few roots for blanching at weekly intervals, a continuous supply of chicons can be had throughout the winter.

I use my own garden soil as the growing medium as it is on the light side, but a little sand or peat should be added to a heavier soil or alternatively use a potting compost. For perfect blanching, growth must be made in complete darkness. It only needs a chink of light to cause greening and a bitter taste to develop. Plant five or six roots upright in a 20- or 23-cm (8- or 9-in) pot, making sure that 1cm (½in) of each crown is above the surface; water gently and cover. A slightly larger pot inverted makes a good cover providing the drainage holes are blocked to prevent any entry of light. Keep the growing medium damp but never wet for overwatering brings with it the risk of rotting. This is about the only disease problem to be considered.

I force in the cellar which has a fairly constant temperature and is almost dark anyway, but any airy place where a temperature of 7.5 to 13°C (45 to 55°F) is maintained is ideal. Under such conditions the blanched chicons are ready for use in four to five weeks.

Varieties

Witloof: is the best known variety for forcing with success.

Endive

Endive is invaluable for late-summer and winter salads. It is related to chicory and shares the need for blanching.

Sowing and growing

Choose a warm sunny site and sow very thinly any time from April to August in 1-cm (½-in) deep drills spaced 38cm (15in) apart. A sowing following the lifting of early potatoes does well, but varieties with deeply curled leaves tend to rot quickly under blanching conditions so are best suited to the earlier sowings. When the seedlings are large enough to handle thin out to 30cm (12in) between plants. Drought encourages the plants to run to seed so water well during dry spells.

Blanching

When plants are obviously full sized they are ready for blanching. Deal with only a few plants at a time as once fully blanched they will not keep in good condition for very long. Some success is achieved by bunching the plant together and tying it round with raffia but this will only blanch the heart. All light must be excluded for complete blanching.

A more satisfactory method is to cover a plant with an upturned plastic pot large enough to enclose the leaves without packing them in tightly. This makes an ideal cover but remember to cover the drainage holes to exclude light and weigh the pot down at the same time using a large stone. Start the operation when both plant and soil are dry as any dampness causes rotting.

Cut endive for immediate use as soon as the whole plant is blanched to a creamy white.

Varieties

Batavian Green: this is suitable for later sowings in July and August. It can be used as a winter salad or cooked.

Moss Curled: best sown early, in April.

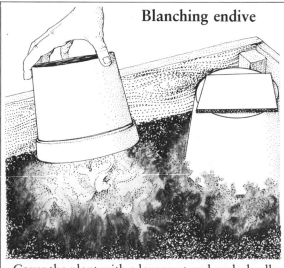

Blanching endive

Cover the plant with a large pot and exclude all light

Mustard and Cress

Mustard and cress can be grown all the year round given a minimum temperature of around 10°C (50°F). For the two to be ready together sow the cress first and the mustard three or four days later.

Fill a seed tray with seed-sowing compost, level it and sprinkle the seed evenly over the surface. Leave the seed exposed and water in using a fine rose. Keep the trays in the dark until the seed leaves open out (they can be covered with several sheets of newspaper). Early in the season they can be grown on the greenhouse bench, but during the spring and

A curly-leaved endive

summer the trays can stand outside.

The crop is ready for cutting about three weeks after sowing when the leaves are fully green. Mustard and cress can be grown with success on a windowsill or in shallow containers on the patio.

Radish

Radish is a quick and easy crop to grow and specially suitable for inter-cropping.

When to sow
An early sowing can be made in the greenhouse border but for my first spring radishes I prepare a fine seed-bed in a cold frame and sow very thinly, raking the seed in lightly afterwards. With the seed evenly distributed they have plenty of room to swell. It is important to sow thinly as where there is overcrowding only thin roots will be produced. Cherry Belle and French Breakfast suit this sowing well.

Once soil conditions improve radishes are ready for pulling four weeks from sowing. To ensure a continuous supply of first-class roots sow in short rows 1cm (½in) deep at fortnightly intervals. Sowing a packet of mixed seed gives a variety of shapes and colours, but whatever the variety all radishes should be pulled while young; with age they go pithy and hollow. Clear away any radishes left standing past their best as they could be a breeding ground for cabbage root fly.

Winter radish
Hardy winter radish can be sown in August. Thin to 8cm (3in) apart and leave in the ground for winter use, to pull as required. They may need to be protected with a layer of straw in severe weather.

Varieties
Cherry Belle: a round red radish of mild flavour. Sow from March to September.
French Breakfast: suitable for early sowings; half red, half white in colour.
Red Globe: red in colour, crisp in texture.
Winter Radishes
Black Spanish: large, round and black. Peel the skin to expose the white flesh.
China Rose: very large, cylindrical root.

Mustard (right), cress (left)
and radish Red Globe

Cucumbers

Cucumbers can be grown all the year round under glass if heat is provided. But for me the cost of greenhouse heating during the winter months is too high, so I wait until March.

Sowing

I then sow single seeds in 8-cm (3-in) pots, filled with moistened peat-based seed compost. Put the seed on its edge ½cm (¼in) deep. Then give one watering using a fine rose. This will be sufficient for the germination period which should be about four to five days in a propagating frame kept at 18.5°C (65°F). Good germination can be achieved on the kitchen windowsill but once the seedlings are through more light is needed so move to the greenhouse if possible.

From March onwards it is relatively easy to maintain the essential warm and humid growing conditions. To avoid overcrowding on the greenhouse bench space the seedlings further apart from time to time. March-sown seedlings will be ready for planting out in the cold greenhouse at the end of April. I make a second sowing in April for planting out in the cold frame once it is safe to do so, usually by the last two weeks of May. These plants will then be cropping when the earlier ones are exhausted.

Planting

I would prefer to plant into a mound made up of well-rotted strawy farmyard manure

Plant ridge cucumbers on a slight mound

covered with soil, but failing that a mound of well-rotted compost would be suitable. Peat growing bags are a good alternative and provide a warmer medium than the soil. Only plant two to a bag; allowing generous spacing gives plenty of air movement round the plants and this will pay off in the end by giving less problems with diseases associated with stagnant air.

In the greenhouse I place the growing bags lengthways, 30cm (1ft) from the side. Supporting wires, canes or netting are easily fixed to the roof and after planting the mainstem is tied loosely to the chosen support. A strong plant can be allowed to grow up and be stopped at the greenhouse ridge.

Stopping laterals

Stop after the third leaf has formed. It is on the laterals that fruiting takes place

Training

For successful cropping correct training and care is essential. Remove all flowers from the mainstem allowing fruits to develop on the laterals only. These will have a better flavour. Shorten the laterals to two or three leaf joints and when necessary tie in the laterals for support. Remove all the male flowers before they open so that there can be no fertilisation of the female flowers. If fertilisation does occur, swollen fruits full of large seeds are formed which can be bitter to the taste. You can always recognise a female flower for there is an embryo cucumber behind it, whereas there is only a thin stem behind a male flower. All female-flowered varieties can fruit on the

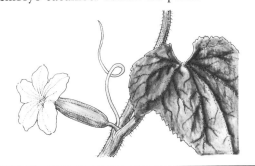

The female flower can be recognised by the embryo cucumber behind the petals

A good crop of cucumbers growing in the greenhouse

mainstem and there are no male flowers to be taken off, but so far I have found their quality inferior.

In the cold frame I train as above but horizontally, not vertically, along a cane from the plant which is at the high end along the ground towards the lower end. I then pinch out the tip when it reaches the edge of the frame.

Care and cultivation
In all situations start feeding about a month after planting out with a liquid organically-based fertiliser applied at fortnightly intervals. Avoid using inorganic fertilisers as their use is one of the causes of bitterness.

Cucumbers can suffer from a type of blossom-end rot if they are ever short of water, so make sure you water adequately so there is never a sign of wilting. In the greenhouse give a fine overhead spray of clear water at midday to keep up the humidity level; a dry hot atmosphere encourages red spider mite whose attentions all too soon turn healthy functioning green leaves into useless yellow ones.

Cucumbers are very sensitive to direct sunlight, foliage near the glass, particularly in a cold frame, is liable to scorch, so shading is advisable for both frame and greenhouse.

Ridge cucumbers
Today's ridge cucumber varieties such as Long Green and Burpless Tasty Green are well worth growing. I sow in April, germinating the seeds in 8-cm (3-in) pots in the propagating frame. Then I grow them on indoors until safe to plant outside at the end of May. Plant about 1m (3ft) apart into a pocket of well-rotted compost leaving a shallow depression around each plant for easy watering. It is advisable to keep the plants under cloches for the first ten days or so.

I let the plants wander over the ground without stopping or pinching out and feed at fortnightly intervals with an organic fertiliser. I treat pickling cucumbers the same as ridge cucumbers and have found the varieties Prolific and Venlo Pickling satisfactory.

Varieties
Femspot: this is an F_1 hybrid only bearing female flowers. It crops heavily and suitable for the greenhouse or the frame.
Telegraph Improved: superb quality fruits; grows well in the greenhouse or a frame. Remember to remove the male flowers.

Ridge
Burpless Tasty Green: an F_1 hybrid which should be grown in a frame although it will succeed outside in the south.
Long Green: a heavy cropper of good flavour that can be grown in a frame or out of doors.

Lettuce

Homegrowing cuts down lettuce's worst enemies: time and travel. With only the short journey from garden to kitchen the fresh crispness of well-chosen varieties is quite something. Lettuce is easy to grow on almost any soil with good drainage.

Preparing the soil
For outdoor growing prepare a fine tilth and if possible cash in on the organic residues of manure applied for a previous crop. Poor results in lettuce growing are often due to ground having been manured too recently. The addition of peat during the winter digging, however, provides a neutral organic content that will give the increased moisture-holding capacity required for the hot summer months but with no adverse effects. Choose an open sunny site, for in the shade heart formation and growth are poor. Apply a light dressing of garden lime if the soil is on the acid side.

An early crop
For the earliest crop outside I sow Fortune in February very thinly and only lightly covered in a pan of seed-sowing compost. The seed germinates quickly at a temperature of 13°C (55°F) in the propagating frame. As soon as the seedlings can be handled I prick them out into trays of potting compost, spacing them 5cm (2in) apart or singly into small peat pots.

By mid-March the seedlings are ready for hardening off in the cold frame and then at the end of March I plant out under cloches. Place the cloches in position a week or so beforehand to warm up the soil and dry it out a little. I plant two rows 23cm (9in) apart with 23cm (9in) between plants. Leave a 1-cm (½-in) space between cloches to allow ventilation and so reduce the risk of disease.

Growing outdoors
By early April it should be possible to prepare a seed bed for direct sowing outdoors. If soil fertility is low rake in a light dressing of Growmore fertiliser. It is best to prepare a seed bed when the soil is dry on top and moist underneath. Always sow very thinly in shallow drills and cover with no more than ½cm (¼in) of fine soil. Sowing too deeply is a common cause of poor germination. Sowing during hot weather when the temperature is continuously over 18.5°C (65°F) also gives bad results.

Thin out as soon as possible to a distance suitable to the variety. That quality giant Webb's Wonderful demands a 30cm (12in) spacing whereas the compact cos-type Little Gem does very well only 15cm (6in) apart. For a supply of good hearted lettuces throughout the summer sow short rows at two to three week intervals. Summer lettuces mature quickly enabling the rows to be fitted in between rows of slower growing crops such as brassicas or celery.

Thinnings pulled when they are between 3 and 5cm (1 and 2in) tall with good undamaged roots transplant well early in the season. However, after mid-summer the move encourages too many cases of bolting to seed; from then on it should be direct sowing only. There is a greater chance of bolting in hot dry weather but artificial watering helps to lessen

the problem. Little Gem and the cabbage-type Continuity, with its attractive bronze-edged leaves, are favourites of mine anyway but their ability to stand for a long while in good condition during a hot spell should please everyone.

Late cropping

For late-autumn cutting I sow the hardy cos-type Winter Density outside in July. A further sowing in October if given cloche protection after Christmas can extend harvesting into March or even April if the winter is mild. Thin out to 25cm (10in) apart so the air can circulate well around the plants. Stagnant cold air suits the fungus disease botrytis (grey mould) literally down to the ground. Mouldy patches start on the underside of the leaves and spread eventually to the whole of the plant.

Cold winter weather and protection give a higher risk of disease. The safeguard is ventilation. Remember to leave a 1-cm (½-in) space between the cloches and give a crack of air to the cold frame as often as the weather allows. Actual watering is unlikely to be necessary during the winter and early spring; growing on the dry side is all to the good.

From left to right: Little Gem, Continuity, Windermere and Salad Bowl

Varieties

Arctic King: a winter lettuce for growing outside in September and October for harvesting in spring. Very hardy, compact in form. Not suitable for spring sowings.

Avondefiance: resistant to mildew disease. Most suitable lettuce for sowing from June to August.

Continuity: outer leaves edged with bronze; a quality lettuce for sowing in spring.

Fortune: a superb lettuce for early sowing in the greenhouse and transplating outside. Can be sown directly outside in March.

Little Gem: a cos-type lettuce; crisp and full of flavour. Stands well in dry periods without bolting. Sow outside from March to July.

Salad Bowl: a large non-hearting lettuce from which leaves are picked as the need arises. Does not run to seed, so ideal for the small salad eater.

Webb's Wonderful: a crisp lettuce with a large heart. The original stock is no longer available.

Windermere: a large crisp lettuce that can be sown outside from March to July.

Winter Density: a cos lettuce of fine quality. Sow in autumn for a spring harvest. Can also be sown in spring.

Tomatoes

If the rules are kept tomato growing is not difficult. The first rule is to choose a variety that suits not only your taste but also the environment in which it is going to be raised. For the greenhouse I look for a compact plant that is short stemmed between the flower trusses and therefore capable of ripening plenty of fruit before reaching the greenhouse roof. In addition good flavour and cropping capacity, reasonable disease resistance and freedom from greenback (failure to ripen at the shoulder of the fruit) are essentials. Varieties which pass on all counts in practice are the ones I stay with, for no amount of growing skill can improve a poor variety. For outdoor growing the criteria are not very different and I have found that most varieties that do well indoors also grow well outdoors.

Sowing

For growing in the greenhouse I sow in early February. To succeed, growth must be steady without a check from seedling stage to fruiting and that could be difficult from an earlier sowing. I sow thinly in a 9-cm (3½-in) pot of seed sowing compost and cover lightly, then water using a fine rose on the can. Germination will only take a few days in a propagating frame kept at 15 to 18.5°C (60 to 65°F).

Prick out tomato seedlings as soon as the seed leaves straighten out, failure to do this spoils the chances of a large first truss of flowers. I prick out into 8-cm (3-in) pots of peat potting compost and space out well on the greenhouse bench so that each plant has adequate light and air as it grows. The greenhouse temperature is kept constantly at a minimum of 10°C (50°F).

Tomato seed germinates well on the kitchen windowsill but when the seedlings are ready for pricking out they must be moved to better light. Otherwise they will be drawn and weak, a condition invariably followed by fruit-setting problems.

Planting

There is usually no soil sickness during the first two or three years of direct planting into the border soil of the greenhouse. However, if there is no break in cropping there will be trouble as time goes on. Diseases, such as verticillium wilt (sleepy disease), and pests, such as tomato eelworm, will build up. Also repeated fertiliser applications may eventually create, rather than solve, feeding problems.

A change of soil may be practical in a small greenhouse but to be effective it must be to a depth of at least 1m (3ft). My present solution is the growing bag, another one is ring culture. In peat growing bags I have found that two plants to a bag give the best return. Three, and certainly four, compete too much for light and air. Good drainage I regard as essential so I make small slits low down in the sides of the bag. I train a single stem for fruiting, twisting it carefully round strong double 6-ply fillis running from a stake in the ground up to a thick cross wire above.

General care

The setting of the first truss is uncertain so I spray once with a tomato fruit-setting spray. Start feeding with a high-potash liquid fertiliser according to the manufacturer's instructions when the first truss sets and repeat at weekly intervals. Nip out all side shoots as soon as they appear.

Watering calls for on-the-spot judgement. Over-watering is bad, but shortage of water, however temporary, causes the dark sunken patches of blossom end rot to appear on the fruit a few weeks later. Watering the greenhouse path at midday helps to keep up

Take out side shoots of tomatoes as soon as they appear

humidity and discourages red spider mite.

At about the three-truss stage calcium deficiency can cause flower drop. I give a precautionary watering with a small handful of hydrated lime stirred well into 9 litres (2 gal) of water at this time. The best insurance against fungal diseases is good ventilation particularly at ground level. Defoliating the stem progressively as the fruit ripens (never remove leaves ahead of a ripening truss) also aids air movement at ground level.

Growing outdoors

I plant Alicante outside 45cm (18in) apart in May in a sheltered, full-sun position. Before planting work in some well-rotted compost and then with cloche protection until June a good start is ensured. With a strong cane for support I train up a single stem to four or five

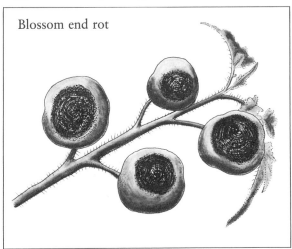

Blossom end rot

trusses before stopping. Feeding is the same as for indoors, once a week with a liquid fertiliser. Remember to remove all side shoots, water well and hope for a sunny summer.

Full-sized fruit still green in September will ripen indoors on a windowsill or in a box kept in dry, well-ventilated place.

Pests and diseases

Whitefly is a serious pest of tomatoes growing in the greenhouse. Spray with a safe insecticide such as malathion, at twice-weekly intervals. Blackbirds are a pest on colouring fruit in the garden; it may be necessary to net plants growing in the open. For other pest and disease problems see the chart on page 71.

Chlorotic patches between the veins denote magnesium deficiency. This is often accompanied by the leaf margins rolling upwards

Varieties
Greenhouse
Ailsa Craig: Makes a large plant, with fruits full of flavour but subject to greenback.
Alicante: Excellent flavour; heavy cropper. Suitable for the small greenhouse.
Golden Queen: Yellow fruits must be picked as soon as they colour. Very sweet.
Moneymaker: Heavy cropper but bears fine fruits with little flavour.
Tigerella: Fruits striped red and yellow, good flavour. Large plant.

Outdoors
Alicante: equally suitable for growing outside as in the greenhouse.
The Amateur: A bush variety with fine quality fruits.
Sigmabush: F_1 hybrid does well in poor seasons. A bush variety with fruits of good flavour.

ROOT CROPS

In various ways nature organises the laying down of food reserves against the winter, so that plants can survive in good health and are, in most cases, ready to produce seed the following season. By harvesting root crops we are cashing in on a top class survival system and if our planning is good we step in just when the valuable reserves are at their greatest and most palatable. Given the chance, nearly all root crops are biennials. This implies a good storage potential without even seeing the roots, for instance of parsnips or celeriac, out of the ground.

To have highly nutritious root vegetables just right for eating all the year round only requires good ground preparation and careful choice of varieties and sowing times. I start with the ground dug in autumn and conditioned by winter winds, rain and frost. A well-prepared seed bed is essential and so much harder to achieve if the digging is left until spring. Roots are best grown on ground to which well-rotted manure or compost was added for the previous season's crop; on freshly-manured land roots that are meant to be straight tend to be forked and thinner.

Jerusalem Artichokes

The tubers remind those who like them of roasted chestnuts; by others they are regarded as too earthy. I think the taste is worth acquiring. They are easy to grow, almost any soil will do and the plants will even thrive in shade. The tall summer foliage of a double row makes an ideal screen for an unsightly corner of the vegetable garden such as round the compost bin.

Some well-rotted compost dug in during the previous winter increases the number and size of the tubers. Only plant freshly-dug tubers, as they dry and shrivel quickly out of the earth. In February plant tubers 10cm (4in) deep and 30cm (12in) apart with 60cm (2ft) between rows. After planting little care is needed until in October the tops turn yellow and die down. From then on until the end of March or beginning of April lift just as many and often as required.

As my growing site is permanent I keep my stock going strongly by putting back one or two of the best quality tubers each time I lift. When the site is cleared in spring give the row an application of Growmore fertiliser.

Beetroot

A light to medium soil suits beetroot best but heavier types can become suitable if thoroughly worked; however, do not attempt to grow in shade. For the best texture and

Golden Beet, a change from the traditional crimson varieties

Sowing and Harvesting Chart

Crop	When to sow in the open	When to sow under glass	When to plant out	Distance between plants	Distance between rows	When to harvest
Jerusalem Artichokes			February	30cm (12in)	60cm (2ft)	October - March
Beetroot	April - July			20cm (8in)	38cm (15in)	July - October
Carrots	March - July	November - February		2.5-10cm (1-4in)	30cm (12in)	April - October
Celeriac		April	May - June	30cm (12in)	45cm (18in)	October - February
Parsnip	February - March			23cm (9in)	45cm (18in)	November - March
Swede	May - July			30cm (12in)	45cm (18in)	October - December
Turnip	April - July	February - March		15cm (6in)	30cm (12in)	June - November
Potatoes earlies			March	30cm (12in)	75cm (2ft 6in)	June - July
maincrop			March - April	38cm (15in)	75cm (2ft 6in)	September
Onions seed	March - April	January	April	20cm (8in)	30cm (12in)	August - September
sets			March	23cm (9in)	30cm (12in)	August
Japanese onions	August			13-15cm (5-6in)	30cm (12in)	July - August
Salad onions	March - September				30cm (12in)	March - October
Shallots			December - January	15cm (6in)	30cm (12in)	June - July

flavour beetroot should be pulled when it is young and small, so ensure a long supply of tender beetroot by making successional sowings at monthly intervals throughout the growing season. They can also be stored successfully for winter use.

Sowing

Early sowings tend to run to seed so I do not start until mid-April. For my first row I sow Boltardy. This variety is least likely to bolt and is my choice for sowings up to mid-July. From then on and for storage, I sow the

Thinning beetroot

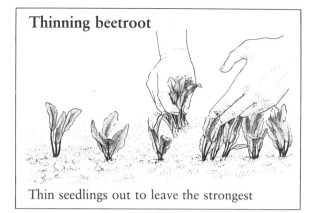

Thin seedlings out to leave the strongest

dependable Detroit Little Ball with the occasional contrast of a short row of Golden Beet.

Sow in drills 2.5cm (1in) deep and 38cm (15in) apart. Beet has a cluster-type seed from which several seedlings are produced, so to save work and seed I place the clusters singly 20cm (8in) apart along the drill. This allows for selection of the strongest seedling at each position and leaves them correctly spaced in the row.

Storing

I have often been disappointed by beetroot stored in the traditional way in boxes of dry sand as the roots have tended to shrivel before they were needed for use. I prefer to store them in a hole in the ground lined with straw and covered with more straw and a few inches of soil. After pulling, whether for immediate use or storage, lay the beet on the ground for a day or so to wilt the tops, then screw them off; this will prevent 'bleeding'.

Varieties

Boltardy: globe-shaped roots with dark crimson flesh. Resistant to bolting so suitable for early-spring planting.
Cheltenham Green Top: a long root of deep-red colour and good flavour.
Detroit Little Ball: a small globular beet. Best for successional sowing.
Golden Beet: golden flesh has a fine flavour.

Storing beetroot

Screw off the tops to avoid bleeding

Pile roots for storing in a straw-lined depression

Complete the clamp with a layer of beaten earth

Carrots

Carrots do best on light to medium soils but thorough winter cultivation can make good results possible on heavier types. What is needed is a deep open-textured soil to allow development of the long tap root of the carrot. There must be no pan of hard sub-soil to stop the root going straight down.

Preparing the soil

I regard deep winter digging carried out before Christmas as essential for getting the right conditions for carrots. Forked roots will be a problem after freshly applying organic manures, so try to follow a crop for which manure was applied the previous season. A general fertiliser worked in when the seed bed is prepared should supply the crops with nutrients throughout the growing period without any further additions.

When to sow

Very early carrots can be grown under glass.

For sowing in the greenhouse border or in the cold frame from November till February choose a variety specially recommended for early forcing, such as Amsterdam Forcing-Amstel or Early Nantes. The worst problem, carrot fly, does not occur under glass.

I make my first outdoor sowing for summer use at the end of March or early April, depending on the weather. There are two reasons for poor or zero germination: they are wet and cold soil in spring and very hot and dry conditions at the height of summer. So sowing should not be carried out when these conditions prevail.

Sowing

Time is needed to prepare a good seed bed, raking and firming the surface at intervals over a few days. It is ready for sowing when the top tilth is fine and dry with some moisture underneath. I make a shallow drill no more than 1cm (½in) deep using the back corner of the rake. It is hard to go too deep with the rake; sowing too deeply is the most common cause of germination failure. Sow very thinly so that the minimum of thinning out is needed.

I sprinkle bromophos granules along the open drill as a first defence against the carrot fly, for without some action the larvae can make the crop useless.

Successional sowing for immediate use goes on till mid-July. I sow my maincrop for winter use early in June. Earlier sowings mature too early to cope with the pressure of taking up the late summer rains without cracking. A carrot which is still growing and flexible in late summer can take advantage of the rain and increase its size with rarely a crack.

Ease up carrots with a fork to facilitate harvesting

Thinning

For pulling as young summer carrots I thin early to 3cm (1in) apart in the row. Maincrop should be given more space, so thin to 10cm (4in) apart. The carrot fly is attracted by the smell of bruised carrot foliage when it is looking for an egg-laying site, so after thinning I water along the row with gamma HCH.

Harvesting and storing

I prefer what I call natural storage. That is the way nature intended, leaving them in the ground for use as required. I have so often been disappointed bringing dry shrivelled or rotten carrots out of clamps or boxes of sand. Once it is lifted the carrot is very prone to fungal and bacterial diseases. The deciding factor to me regarding lifting or not lifting would be the question of drainage and the slug problem on a heavy soil.

Varieties

Amsterdam Forcing-Amstel: can be sown in a frame or greenhouse for an early crop or in the open for succession. A stump rooted variety the size of a finger.
Chantenay Red Cored–Favourite: an excellent stump-rooted main crop variety, ideal for storage.
Early Nantes: a blunt-ended variety for

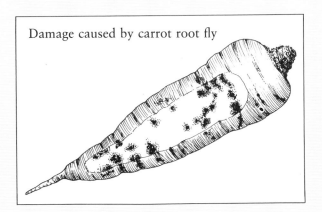
Damage caused by carrot root fly

forcing. Good flavour.
New Red Intermediate: a long pointed carrot suitable for the show bench. Stores well, of good colour.

Celeriac

Celeriac is the stump-rooted version of celery, its bulbous root swelling just above ground has an excellent celery flavour which is invaluable for winter use.

Sowing and growing
Celeriac needs a deeply cultivated moisture-retaining soil to produce the largest and best-keeping roots, make sure that it is never short of water. I sow in a tray of peat sowing compost in April and germinate this in the propagating frame at 16 to 18.5°C (60 to 65°F).

The seedlings are pricked out into a peat potting compost and spaced 5 cm (2 in) apart for growing on the greenhouse bench. After hardening off in the cold frame during May, they are planted out on the flat 30 cm (12 in) apart with 45 cm (18 in) between the rows.

Unlike celery, neither a trench nor earthing up are needed. The root keeps in the ground perfectly until February on all but the heaviest soils where it should be lifted and stored in a clamp (see Beetroot p.28).

Pests
The pest to watch for is the celery leaf miner for which I spray with gamma HCH when I see the first sign of the mining trails showing up in the leaves.

Varieties
Globus: a fine root of good flavour.

Parsnips

Here is a first class vegetable with no storage problems, if the soil is well drained the crop will stand in the ground in good condition for use as required until the early spring. I find the flavour is improved after frost. The longest growing season possible is needed to produce the best crop.

A splendid crop of roots and tubers
Left to right: swede, Jerusalem artichokes with onions behind, golden turnips, globe beet, parsnips, carrots and celeriac with potatoes behind in the basket

Soil preparation

This must be thorough and carried out well in advance of sowing. It is similar to that described for carrots (page 28). The greater the depth of open-textured soil for a long straight root to penetrate the better. Again there is the risk of forked, rather than straight, roots being formed in soil that is still rich from recent manuring or incorporation of compost. As for carrots, it is best to follow on from a crop which received manure or compost before planting.

Sowing

Ideally sow in February but if the ground is too cold and wet sowing must be delayed, both for the production of a good enough seed bed and for the arrival of conditions favourable for satisfactory germination. I advise you to buy new parsnip seed each year as its viability is short lived. Sow in shallow drills 1cm (½in) deep and 45cm (18in) apart. Sow at stations, placing three seeds at 23cm (9in) intervals in the row.

Care and cultivation

When the seedlings are large enough it is easy to thin out by removing all but the strongest seedling at each station. Regular weeding and watering, if necessary, should be all there is left to do; but if in June the parsnips are backward due to a poor start, they will benefit considerably from a foliar feed.

Parsnip canker

Parsnip canker, which rots the roots at the shoulder, is a problem on some soils. There is no cure but where there is a known problem, a variety with a degree of canker resistance, such as Avonresister, should be chosen. It is wise to weed and hoe carefully amongst parsnips so as not to damage the shoulder and thereby invite the entry of the fungi and bacteria which precedes canker. If canker recurs, try sowing a little later than usual next season.

Varieties

Avonresister: resistant to parsnip canker; smaller roots than most other varieties.
Tender and True: a long-rooted variety slightly resistant to parsnip canker. Fine quality and excellent flavour.
White Gem: a short-rooted variety suitable for growing in shallower soils. Very good flavour.

Swedes

The swede is difficult to grow well in a small enclosed garden because of its susceptibility to mildew. Open windy fields are much healthier for it. The risk of infection is reduced by not sowing too early, try June or even July in the south if a May sowing has previously met with failure. The swede is a brassica and therefore subject to clubroot, so it must be grown within the brassica section of the crop rotation scheme.

Sowing and growing
Being a brassica the swede benefits from a light application of hydrated lime raked in before sowing. The seed should be thinly sown, 2cm (¾in) deep between May and July. As soon as the seedlings emerge I dust along the row with derris dust to guard against flea beetle which is liable to ruin a whole row, especially in dry hot weather.

Later thin the young plants to 30cm (12in) apart. This generous spacing will help to improve the chances of a good crop. As a mildew preventative spray with a fungicide, zineb or liquid copper, in late August.

I prefer to leave swedes in the ground over winter but with a wet heavy soil I would have to consider a clamp for storage.

Varieties
Marian: forms roots of excellent quality.
Purple Top: a large swede of fine flavour.

Turnips

Turnips are easy to grow but it must be remembered that, like swedes, they are brassicas and must be planted in the same crop rotation section as cabbages.

When to sow
For an early crop sow Jersey Navet in the cold frame in late February or early March. Old turnips are coarse and peppery but pulled young, the size of golf balls, they are delicious. To ensure a constant supply sow short rows of Snowball outdoors every three weeks or so, from April onwards. These sowings can be continued till early August giving a continuous supply of tender young roots all through the summer and early autumn. The hardier Golden Ball sown in June or July is a good choice for autumn use and winter storage.

Sowing and growing
Turnips like to be firm in the ground, so make a firm seed bed or, if sowing after a previous crop, rake the soil lightly and let it settle before sowing. As for all brassicas, rake in a light dressing of hydrated lime when preparing the bed. Sow 2cm (¾in) deep in drills 30cm (12in) apart thinning out to 15cm (6in) apart in the row. If the seedlings emerge in hot dry weather dust along the row with derris dust to guard against flea beetle.

Wait for maturity before lifting turnips for storage which should be carried out as for beetroots (see page 28).

Varieties
Golden Ball: yellow flesh, stores well.
Jersey Navet: cylindrical roots of good flavour. Best for early sowings.
Snowball: white flesh of mild flavour.

Onions

Onions are gross feeders demanding a soil enriched with well-rotted manure or well-made compost. Apply as much as possible during the winter digging. I favour a permanent site where the level of fertility increases and the weed problem gets less from season to season, only soil-borne diseases such as white rot and eelworm would make me move. In preparation for sowing and transplanting I make an overall application of meat and bone meal at 100g per sq m (3oz per sq yd) in March and then break down the top surface with a three-pronged cultivator.

Sowing and thinning
I look to direct sowing to provide keepers, choosing well tried varieties such as Bedfordshire Champion, Improved Reading or Solidity. A really firm seed-bed is essential. Take time over it, raking and firming at intervals of a few days to get it just right. Sow

Planting onion sets

Plant with a trowel 23cm (9in) apart against a garden line

in drills 30cm (12in) apart no deeper than 1cm (½in) and sprinkle the open drill with bromophos granules as a precaution against onion fly. Sow very thinly along the row. Never pull onions from the main bed for salad use as this will attract the onion fly.

Specially prepared onion sets avoid the onion fly problem. Sets should be planted firmly with a trowel keeping the tip just above the ground. Plant 23cm (9in) apart in the row with 30cm (12in) between rows in March for lifting in August.

Care and cultivation

Early on weeds can smother onion seedlings, while in the growing season they compete for the extra nutrients and moisture applied. Also sunshine is needed to ripen the bulbs and weeds will stop the sun at harvest time. The traditional swan-necked hoe is just the tool for weeding without doing damage to the young bulbs. Do not feed any onions for keeping after mid-July, overstimulation from then on impairs keeping qualities.

In August or September when the swelling of the bulbs is complete, any tops which have not fallen over naturally can gently be bent over so that all the bulbs are exposed to the sun. This bend will slow down the sap flow to the leaf, the root system is then de-activated and ripening begins in earnest.

Storing

After a week or so the onions are ready for lifting and drying off completely. String onions up and hang in an airy frost-free place and check regularly for any rot. Onions can be dusted with flowers of sulphur to prevent rotting.

Large onions

Large onions weighing 1.6kg (3lb) or over, need an early start with heat. I like to sow large varieties such as Ailsa Craig and Improved Mammoth on the first day of January, germinating the seed in the greenhouse propagator at 16°C (60°F). I prick the seedlings out singly into 9-cm (3½-in) pots using peat potting compost, while they are still in the loop stage (green parts bent over like a hair pin). Any delay causes a growth check and affects the ultimate size.

Never allow a shortage of water, but take care as overwatering leads to damping off. This causes the seedlings to topple over and shrivel. If this happens water or spray with benomyl as directed on the packet. My seedlings grow on under cool conditions in the greenhouse and are finally hardened off in the cold frame for planting out in mid-April. Planting is according to expected size, but 20 to 25cm (8 to 10in) apart in the row and a gap of 30 to 38cm (12 to 15in) between rows is a good average. Large onions are made simply of larger cells boosted by an early start and a plentiful supply of food and water throughout the growing season. They do not keep.

Varieties

Ailsa Craig: large onion; can be sown in the greenhouse and transplanted outside in spring or sown directly outside in March.
Bedfordshire Champion: very good keeper.
Blood Red: good keeper; firm red onion.
Improved Mammoth: a huge onion suitable for exhibition. Sow in the greenhouse and transplant outside in spring.
Improved Reading: a good keeper; sow directly outside. Flat shape.
Solidity: good keeper for sowing outside.
Stuttgarter Giant: flat onion of mild flavour; good keeper. Can be grown from sets.

Japanese Onions

These are the latest addition to the list of varieties. They are sown in open ground in August and over-wintered in the drill. The thinnings can be used early in the spring as salad onions, leaving the remaining onions 13 to 15cm (5 to 6in) apart in the row. Care and cultivation during the growing season is as for spring sown onions. These onions are ready for lifting in July and August. They are good keepers and have a mild flavour.

Varieties
Express Yellow: good keeping onion; flat in shape. Sow during August.
Kaizuka Extra Early: pale-yellow onion for an August sowing.

Shallots

Shallots are the ideal onion for pickling but they need a long growing season to do their best. Plant shallots with a trowel 15cm (6in) apart as early in the year as possible and as soon as the ground is dry enough. A single bulb multiplies six or eight fold by harvesting time in June or July.

Shallots ripening in the sun

Varieties
Giant Yellow: fine pickling onion; harvest in June.
Long-Keeping Yellow: keeps well, good flavour, suitable for pickling.

Potatoes

Potatoes are recommended for cleaning ground but it is the cultivation involved that makes the improvement. To have a succession of healthy crops, potatoes must stay strictly in line with the basic crop rotation plan and not appear on the same land more than once in three years. If this rule is broken there is every likelihood of potato cyst eelworm becoming established in the soil and further potato growing being made impossible for many years. To guard against this problem buy only Ministry of Agriculture Certificated seed, this means a healthy start. I would not recommend the saving of one's own seed for more than one year, however clean and safe the crop looks.

Preparing the soil
Medium soils are the most suitable, but light soils can be improved by the addition of well-rotted organic manures. Heavy soils, with their high slug population and tendency to be wet at lifting time, may well prove too difficult. Choose an open site and dig in plenty of well-rotted compost or manure in the winter. Not only does this provide nutrients and improve the texture and moisture-holding capacity of the soil, but it also supports predacious fungi which are invaluable against potato eelworm. Do not apply lime as it can encourage scab.

Planting
Sprouted or chitted tubers are best for planting so I order early to allow plenty of time for setting them up to sprout. Stand in trays with eyes uppermost in good light and in a place where it is cool but frost free. When planting take care not to damage the sprouts. If seed is short it is worth cutting tubers but each piece must have at least one good eye or sprout. Dust the cut with flowers of sulphur

to prevent rotting and plant immediately.

In March or April I open up a trench 15cm (6in) deep. Place some well-rotted compost to the bottom of the trench to help to ensure a clean crop; also sprinkle in a dressing of Growmore fertiliser. First earlies are planted 30cm (12in) apart with 75cm (2ft 6in) between rows. Later varieties should be planted 38cm (15in) apart again with 75cm (2ft 6in) between rows.

Care and cultivation

Potatoes take up quite a lot of room, but first earlies deserve a place even in a small garden. For this purpose Foremost is a really quick mover early on and combines quality with quantity at lifting time. When the tops are just emerging so that I can see the rows, I go through with a light hand cultivator to break the soil surface. This will let in the air and kill the seedling weeds but it must be superficial to prevent damage to the roots.

Potato tops are frost sensitive so whenever frost is forecast I draw soil over the tops with a draw hoe. When they get too big for that I cover them with whole newspapers during the night but remove them early the following morning. Frosty nights are usually still, so a few clods of earth will keep the papers in place. Tops cut down by the frost are replaced

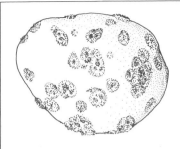

Potato scab
The corky lesions are usually caused by a lack of organic matter in the soil. The potatoes are still edible

but it delays the crop.

When growth is a few inches high I start earthing up. This entails drawing soil up each side of the row. This is repeated so the final ridge is high enough to accommodate a maximum number of cropping roots and preventing greening of tubers near the surface. Any tubers which are green are inedible and should be discarded.

During dry weather water thoroughly to penetrate right down to the roots under the centre of the plants. Water speeds up bulking and increases potato size which adds considerably to the total weight.

Harvesting and storing

To harvest the maincrop for storage choose a dry day, lift the potatoes carefully with a fork and leave them for a few hours on the soil to dry off. Lift every tuber for even the smallest left to grow another year will break the crop rotation rule. Select your tubers for storing, only sound ones are worth keeping. I tuck mine away inside a straw-lined clamp with a wisp of straw acting as a ventilator poking out through the top. Cover over the tubers with straw and then a layer of beaten earth about 23cm (9in) thick.

Varieties
Earlies
Duke of York: excellent flavour; cream flesh.
Foremost: round tubers of fine flavour.
Sharpe's Express: superb flavour.

Maincrop
Desirée: red-skinned tubers with cream flesh; crops heavily, fine flavour.
Majestic: good cropper; excellent for chips.
Pink Fir Apple: excellent for potato salad.

Harvesting early potatoes

LEGUMES

The legumes are an unique group of crops as they leave the soil after cropping richer in nitrogen. On the roots of leguminous plants there are little white nodules containing nitrifying bacteria whose activities turn these nodules, in effect, into miniature nitrogen factories. The bacteria need alkaline surroundings if they are to function properly so apply a light dressing of hydrated lime if the soil is acid before sowing or planting for all leguminous plants.

Thorough winter digging, incorporating plenty of well-rotted manure or compost, lays the right foundation. From a human nutritional point of view legumes are very valuable for they are the vegetables with a high protein content. In the case of those harvested at complete maturity the protein level is high enough for it to be made the heart of a meal in place of the usual animal protein.

Broad Beans

Broad beans would be more popular if they were always picked young. Once they are old they are tough skinned and unpalatable. They are one of the earliest vegetables and with a careful choice of varieties the season can be long; up to six months is possible.

Windsor and longpod
There are two main varieties the shorter-podded Windsors and the longpod varieties which will stand the winter. The Windsor varieties are less hardy and should not be sown until the spring. There are white-seeded and green-seeded varieties amongst both types but there is little difference in taste. The flavour difference lies between the Windsors and the longpods, the former coming out the winner.

Overwintering
Of the longpod varieties which will stand the winter best, Aquadulce is ideally suited for a November sowing and will come through severe frost without harm. Cold soil standing wet for long periods is a worse hazard and provides just the conditions for a high incidence of fungal diseases. So as well as choosing a sheltered, well-drained site it is wise to dress seed which is to be sown during the damp cold months with a fungicidal seed dressing to protect against soil-borne diseases.

A not-so-hardy dwarf variety, The Sutton for example, does well sown in the autumn if given cloche protection after Christmas or a little earlier. With a potential height of no more than 45cm (18in) the protection will not be outgrown while it is needed. I have sown The Sutton successfully in all months of the year; the beans set very readily and have superb flavour every time.

Sowing and growing
I sow all dwarf varieties in single drills 5cm (2in) deep and 38cm (15in) apart. The seeds are spaced 20cm (8in) apart in the drill. Support is rarely needed for dwarf varieties.

I sow tall varieties in double rows so that they are support for each other. The drills are 5cm (2in) deep with the seeds spaced 23cm (9in) apart. I leave from 60cm to 1m (2 to 3ft) between double rows. A few canes and a string or two stretched between them may be needed to keep these plants from flopping over onto neighbouring vegetables. Moisture is essential for good bean setting, so water artificially during dry spells.

Blackfly
Broad beans, particularly those that have overwintered, need watching for blackfly which is first seen in the head of the plant where it settles and multiplies rapidly. If the central growing tip is pinched out as soon as there are plenty of open flowers, the starting

Sowing and Harvesting Chart

Crop	When to sow in the open	When to sow under glass	When to plant out	Distance between plants	Distance between rows	When to harvest
Broad beans	November or February - April			20cm (8in)	38cm (15in)	June - August
French beans	May - July	February	May	30cm (12in)	60cm (2ft)	June - October
Runner beans	mid-May	April	early-June	30cm (12in)	1.5m (5ft) between double rows	July - September
Peas	October - November or March - July	March	May	5cm (2in)	1.2m (4ft) between triple rows	May - October

Blackfly on broad bean

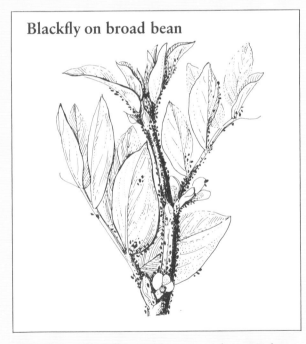

point for a blackfly attack goes with it. With luck this simple approach does the trick, but if blackfly colonies do get established spray with malathion immediately to avoid plant losses.

Varieties
Aquadulce: gives a very early spring crop from a November sowing.
Exhibition Longpod: very long pod filled with good quality white beans.
Midget: a dwarf variety of fine flavour.
The Sutton: A dwarf variety with small beans and pods. Cropping is good and the flavour is excellent.
Unrivalled Green Windsor: sow this green-seeded variety in spring; a good cropper.

French Beans

Dwarf French beans are quick growers and crop earlier than runner beans, no supports are needed but the plants should never be crowded.

An early crop
In mid-February I sow seed singly in small peat pots in the greenhouse which has the required minimum temperature of 13°C (55°F). I then pot on the strongest seedlings into 13-cm (5-in) pots. I prefer to have them in single pots rather than several plants in larger pots. This is because if the plants are well spaced out in good light on the greenhouse bench, with watering, the occasional liquid feed and protection from greenfly they will grow on to crop well indoors.

The early crop could be grown equally well

in the greenhouse border making a drill 5cm (2in) deep with rows 60cm (2ft) apart and the seed spaced every 30cm (12in). Whichever way, I water the greenhouse path to keep up the humidity level and so reduce the risk of red spider mite.

Growing outdoors

When sowing outdoors remember that dwarf French beans just do not like a cold seed bed. It results in poor germination and a low yield from the plants that do manage to emerge. Choose an open site and prepare the ground well. Before sowing or planting I rake in an overall application of Growmore fertiliser at 60g per sq m (2oz per sq yd). The warming up and drying out of the soil can be speeded up by covering the proposed row a week or two beforehand with cloches.

Dwarf French beans are very sensitive to frost so cloches are needed to protect germinated rows and young plants until the risk of frost is over. Plants raised in the greenhouse and planted out give the earliest crop under cloches. Mine go out under protection in the second or third week of May.

In most districts the end of May or the first week in June is plenty early enough for direct sowing in the open without protection. Seed for early sowing should be dressed with a fungicidal dressing. Repeat sowings up to July at two- or three-week intervals. This will give a continuous supply of young beans over a long season.

Dwarf-French-bean flowers develop under the shade of the foliage so they do not suffer, as do those of runner beans, during periods of intense heat and sunlight. As long as regular watering ensures no lack of moisture at the roots they flower and set their beans through the hottest of summers. Watch for blackfly, I spray on sight with a contact insecticide such as malathion, remembering to follow the manufacturer's advice regarding harvesting afterwards.

Climbing French beans are treated as runner beans and are regarded by some to be of a better quality than the traditional runner beans.

The beans are at their best at about 10cm (4in) long, at which size all varieties, not just the stringless ones, will snap in half crisply with no sign of a string.

Varieties

The Prince: very early variety, suitable for growing under cloches.
Kinghorn Waxpod: excellent quality beans if picked when young.
Sprite: my favourite; a really fine flavour.

Runner Beans

The runner bean is one of the most productive vegetables. If managed correctly it will crop continuously and in quantity from July until the first frosts cut the plants down in the autumn.

Preparing the soil

It is essential to prepare the site well in advance of planting, I favour a permanent site where I can build up the right soil conditions over a number of years. Runner beans are very sensitive to drought so it is an efficient moisture-retaining area down below that I am after.

I open up a trench 60cm (2ft) deep and 1m (3ft) wide during the winter and put plenty of organic matter such as well-rotted compost or manure (newspaper or rags could be a substitute) into the bottom. I go along with a dusting of hydrated lime, cover with 15cm (6in) of soil and leave it at that stage for several weeks to weather. I complete the filling in in April, at the same time working in a Growmore fertiliser application of 60g per m (2oz per yd) run of row.

Sowing and planting

For an early start I sow beans singly 5cm (2in) deep in 8-cm (3-in) pots of peat seed-sowing compost in the greenhouse at the end of April. You could alternatively sow into peat pots or soil blocks. The beans are planted out with very little disturbance to the roots, in June when the risk of frost has passed. Space plants 30cm (12in) apart, with 1.5m (5ft) between a double row.

For the earliest crop, plant beans 30cm

Opposite: Runner bean, Enorma, in flower.
Inset top: Broad bean, The Sutton. **Inset bottom:** White-flowered varieties of runner beans set their trusses well

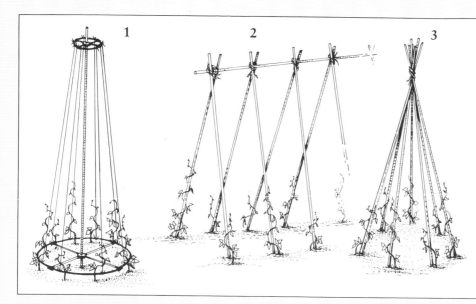

Runner bean supports

1 A maypole arrangement consisting of two wire circles linked by strings

2 A tent consisting of strong poles tied firmly together

3 The wigwam structure should be securely tied at the top

(12in) apart in a single row and successively pinch out the growing tips to make the plants bushy. These are then ground beans with no need for support. They flower and set their beans quickly but the beans form low down and are not very straight but the flavour will be there. The variety Sunset is particularly suited to this treatment.

It is unwise to sow in the open until mid-May as a late frost can easily kill the young seedlings just emerging. The spacing is the same for planting out. It is a good idea to sow a few extras at the end of the row just in case the seeds don't all germinate.

Supports

Runner bean supports should be put in position before planting. There are many ways of arranging them but the important thing is that they should be firm. Beans will not crop well if they and their supports are waving about. Also as the season goes on there are sure to be periods of high wind capable of completely flattening a shakely-built structure. Runner beans are often reluctant to start climbing their supports, so I gently tie in any extension growths that wander. Once they are in close contact they are well away and flowering begins quite low down.

Flower set

First flower trusses have a more-than-usual tendency to drop before any beans are formed. Both acid soil and shortage of phosphate increase the risk of premature flower drop. If the problem occurs, a watering along the row with a handful of hydrated lime stirred into 9 litres (2gals) of water coupled with a foliar feed should bring improvement.

Whenever the weather is dry give a thorough watering, adequate water at the roots is the best aid to flower setting, although spraying with clear water overhead as well may help.

Aphids

Watch for greenfly and blackfly, although the latter is not such a problem as on broad beans. I spray with malathion on sight.

Picking

For a continuous crop of beans the rows must be picked regularly and no beans must ever be allowed to mature. The achievement of fully-ripened beans satisfies the plant and its efforts cease.

Varieties

Achievement: long beans with good flavour; reliable cropper.
Enorma: suitable for the show bench.
Scarlet Emperor: fine flavour; a favourite old variety with a long cropping period.
Sunset: pink flowers that set well; good flavour.
White Achievement: white flowers which set well even in a bad season.

Peas

Most soils that are not acid will grow reasonable pea crops. Improved cropping comes from really thorough pre-planting cultivations and the incorporation of plenty of well-rotted organic matter during the winter. The moisture-holding aspect is most important. If a drought occurs in a dry summer the effect goes right through to the flavour, so water well in dry weather.

Finding pea sticks has become difficult so now I grow mostly the dwarf varieties. A few 1.2m (4ft) canes along the sides of the row and two or three strands of string tied along are sufficient to keep the pods off the ground.

An early crop

An early start can be made by sowing a round-seeded variety such as Feltham First in October or November. The round-seeded peas are hardy and have enough resistance to soil-borne diseases to make autumn sowing worthwhile.

Even so this is a damp cold growing period full of danger for young seedlings; a plant is never stronger than when it is going all out from April onwards with sunshine and temperatures in its favour. For this reason I often sow peas in peat pots filled with a peat-based seed compost early in March and give them the protection of a cold frame after germination in the greenhouse, prior to planting out. Between October and March it is unwise to sow outside without dressing pea seed with a fungicidal seed dressing.

The flavour of the round-seeded peas is nothing compared with that of the sweeter wrinkled-seeded varieties but if picked young they do give a hint of things to come.

Early peas can be brought forward by at least a month by giving them cloche protection. If the cloches are lifted occasionally for weeding, this slight soil disturbance seems to stimulate growth.

Sowing

For sowing I prefer a flat trench, which I draw out 15cm (6in) wide and 5cm (2in) deep. I place three rows of peas on the bottom spaced 5cm (2in) each way. I fill in with fine soil and firm along the length of the row with the back of the rake. In dry weather I soak the peas overnight to encourage germination.

To make the most of the growing season I make a succession of sowings at two to three week intervals until July. Because the sequence works I tend always to start with Feltham First as it is probably the best of the round-seeded peas and follow with Little Marvel which is my idea of what a garden pea should be, then Kelvedon Wonder and Onward.

For a last sowing in July I go back to Kelvedon Wonder which I know is a first early but it is also the variety I have found least susceptible to mildew. This is a disease that has to be reckoned with late in the season and a good autumn crop largely depends on the absence of mildew.

Pea moth

Early peas flowering before June and those flowering after mid-August are rarely affected by pea moth but between those times the female moth is busy laying her eggs in the open pea flowers.

Most insecticides will control the pea moth larvae but I use fenitrothion as this also takes care of aphids, thrips, pea midge and pea weevil. Timing is important, spray in the evening about a week after flowering begins and repeat a fortnight later.

Varieties

I have tried the unusual peas, sugar peas, purple-podded and the French petit pois. But for me they all give too little return in terms of quantity to justify the space they take. The exception is a new variety, Fek. In general I recommend the following:

Feltham First: an early variety suitable for very early sowing, round-seeded, fair quality.
Kelvedon Wonder: an early variety with wrinkled seeds. Resistant to mildew.
Little Marvel: a wrinkled pea of excellent flavour, sow from March onward.
Onward: a wrinkled pea of excellent quality. Good for freezing. Sow from March onward.

BRASSICAS

Amongst the brassicas there is something for everyone's taste and for all seasons. Brassicas are not all just cabbage-like. Think of the difference in look and taste between say Brussels sprouts and calabrese, cauliflower and kohlrabi and you realise how wide the range is. With careful planning this group of vegetables can provide great variety over a year-long season.

All the brassicas should be grown together in a group because they are all susceptible to the fungal disease of clubroot. If this disease builds up in the soil the growing of brassicas on that particular area soon becomes

Club root
This disease affects the roots of brassicas. It is also rather aptly known as finger and toe

hopeless. I know of no worthwhile treatment and once established the trouble remains in the soil for years, maybe a lifetime. The only wise course is to adhere strictly to a rotational growing plan in which brassicas appear no more than once in three years on any one spot. Maybe the visitor's boot is only a low level risk but not so the roots of young plants raised on infected ground elsewhere and

brought in. For this reason I insist on raising my own plants from seed so that they cannot have had any contact with doubtful soil.

The seed bed
I have a well-prepared seed bed set aside specially for sowing all the brassica plants which are to be transplanted as their individual planting time comes along. The rows, only 1m (3ft) long and 30cm (12in) apart, are conveniently sited beside a path where watering, when necessary, is easy and progress can be watched daily. Seedlings must not be crowded or stand too long in the seed bed or they will be drawn and weakly. I sow thinly in 1-cm (½-in) deep drills always remembering to take precautions against cabbage rootfly and never expecting that a particular time of year will save my plants from attack, which it does not.

Preparing the soil
On all but chalky soils hydrated lime should be applied before sowing or planting. I dig as early as possible in the winter and then leave the ground to consolidate, it must be really firm for sowing and planting. Most brassicas are a bit top heavy and need solid ground if their roots are to keep a secure hold. If at planting time the soil has been recently dug I go over it with a three-pronged hand cultivator and then tread it down well with my feet.

Planting
Having prepared a really firm planting area it is important to plant firmly too. It is best to make a planting hole with a dibber and then really firm the plant in with the heel of the boot. Then to ensure the young plant is secure in the ground, pull a leaf tip between the finger and thumb. If the plant moves more firming is necessary; if the leaf tip tears your plant will be off to a good start. Finally, water them in well. When they are established, hoe in a little fertiliser.

Sowing and Harvesting Chart

Crop	When to sow in the open	When to sow under glass	When to plant out	Distance between plants	Distance between rows	When to harvest
Sprouting broccoli	April - May		June - July	75cm (2ft 6in)	1m (3ft)	August - April
Brussels sprouts	April		May - June	75cm (2ft 6in)	1m (3ft)	October - March
Cabbage spring	August		October	45cm (18in)	45cm (18in)	March - June
summer	March - April	February	April - May	60cm (2ft)	60cm (2ft)	May - August
winter	March - April		May - June	60cm (2ft)	60cm (2ft)	September - April
red	April		June	60cm (2ft)	60cm (2ft)	October - February.
Cauliflower summer	March - May	February - March	March - July	60cm (2ft)	60cm (2ft)	June - November
winter	April - May		June - July	60cm (2ft)	60cm (2ft)	January - May
Kale	April - May		June - July	60cm (2ft)	60cm (2ft)	November - April
Kohl rabi	April - June			38cm (15in)	45cm (18in)	July - September

Pests

There are several serious pests to be considered, pigeons are at the top of the list as they can consume a whole crop on one unguarded morning. Not all areas of the country are affected yet but the problem is spreading and the necessity of growing brassicas within a netted cage looms ahead. While the pigeons are not too determined a few canes and single strings at the height of 1m (3ft) across the flight path can work.

Cabbage root fly maggots cause considerable losses among brassica plants. The cabbage root fly lays its eggs just below the soil surface close to the stem of the young plant, when the eggs hatch out the maggots feed on the roots eventually destroying them. Collapse of the plants is sudden and complete, the casualties show up most dramatically

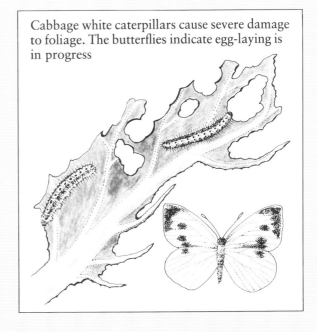

Cabbage white caterpillars cause severe damage to foliage. The butterflies indicate egg-laying is in progress

43

Transplanting brassicas

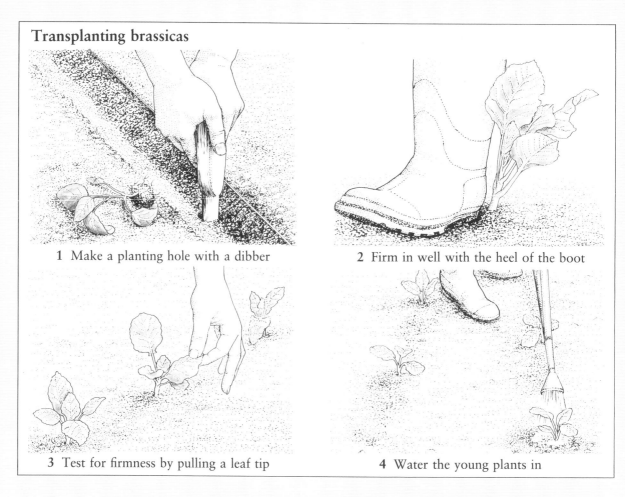

1 Make a planting hole with a dibber

2 Firm in well with the heel of the boot

3 Test for firmness by pulling a leaf tip

4 Water the young plants in

when plants are under stress during dry sunny weather. The placing of felt or plastic discs around the stems at soil level when planting out makes the egg laying site somewhat inaccessible and can be an effective foil, but in practice my discs have always been taken away by badgers — I have yet to understand their interest. As a more reliable measure I apply a few bromophos granules to the dibber holes when planting and afterwards water the plants in with gamma HCH diluted to spraying strength.

Later in the summer large and small cabbage white butterflies and cabbage moths will produce a caterpillar problem if action is not taken as soon as any caterpillars are spotted. Derris, liquid or dust, or fenitrothion take care of caterpillars but treatment should be prompt. Caterpillars have huge appetites and will eat enough to make a crop worthless in a matter of days.

Once a few aphids arrive colonies will be built up quickly. Brussels sprouts seem to be the most popular target where, if they are not disturbed, the aphids will find their way right inside the sprouts. I spray with malathion as soon as I see any aphids on any of the brassicas, giving particular attention to the undersides of the leaves where the colonies are to be found.

Feeding

Brassicas are hungry plants, particularly for nitrogen. Quick growth and good leaf colour are dependant on the nitrogen supply being adequate. Even so, for the sake of overall health, I prefer to give a balanced fertiliser such as Growmore which supplies phosphates and potash in addition to nitrogen. Apart from the delay advisable before feeding spring cabbage, the time to feed is when the plants have settled down after transplanting or thinning.

Sprouting Broccoli

Purple- and, to a lesser extent, white-sprouting broccoli produce an abundance of delicious flowering tips during the difficult period of late winter and early spring. There is the fact to bear in mind that the plants stand on the ground for almost twelve months, but the return in edible crop should be considered to justify the time and space. Two or three plants of the prolific purple-sprouting broccoli are enough for the average family needs.

Purple-sprouting broccoli is the hardiest and heaviest cropper of the group, it will endure cold conditions that are too much for other brassicas. Although impoverished soil will not yield well, and bearing in mind the long standing period over the winter, there is a definite requirement for good drainage. White-sprouting broccoli is less hardy, the flowers form like tiny white cauliflowers for picking March to May.

Sowing and planting
Sow all types in April or May in the seed bed and plant out between June and July. Generous spacing is necessary so leave 75cm (2ft 6in) between plants and 1m (3ft) between rows. Pay special attention to firm planting as broccoli is a tall plant and will not do its best if it rocks about in the wind. Firm in well with the heel of the boot, then test the plant does not move by pulling a leaf tip.

Calabrese
Calabrese is a green-sprouting broccoli. Unlike the others it is early and quick growing. From an April or May sowing the spear-like shoots are ready for picking in August and September. If the shoots are picked while they are still tightly packed, they are deliciously tender with a flavour hinting of asparagus. As they get older they become strong, even bitter, and this may have put some people off what deserves to be a far more popular vegetable.

With all the broccolis the more constant the picking the more there is to follow. Once flowers are allowed to open the production of new shoots slows down and the end of the cropping is in sight.

Varieties
Improved White Sprouting: matures in March and April, less winter-hardy than the purple varieties.
Late Purple Sprouting: crops in April and May, the latest-maturing broccoli.
Purple Sprouting: produces its crop in March and April. A reliable and hardy variety.

Brussels Sprouts

Brussels sprouts are the great winter stand-by, with a picking season stretching from October to March. I sow in the seed bed in mid-April. Sowing earlier means that picking has to start before the main supply of autumn vegetables is over.

Planting
For extra firmness I plant with a dibber rather than with a trowel and firm well in after planting with that best implement, the heel of the boot. In May or early June plant out in rows 1m (3ft) apart with 75cm (2ft 6in) between plants.

Again we have tall plants so firm ground and firm planting are essential if they are to stand securely through the winter without toppling over in the wind. However it is as well to tie each plant of the taller varieties to a

Staking Brussels sprouts

Left to right: Brussels sprout, Peer Gynt; cauliflower, All the Year Round; cabbages, Hispi and White Dutch

cane for support before the worst happens. I choose shorter-growing varieties whenever possible. After the autumn gales Peer Gynt, for example, has a good chance of remaining upright unaided, whereas without help the taller Fillbasket may be laid down from one end of the row to the other. Apart from the nuisance of plants that have toppled over, those which stand firmly without rocking in the wind invariably crop better.

Harvesting
Most F_1 hybrid varieties have been produced for commercial growing by the breeders, the aim being a stem of identical sprouts to get for picking on the same day by mechanical means. In the home-garden situation sprouts maturing progressively over a period of weeks are a better proposition. Two short-stemmed hybrids which do suit me are Peer Gynt and Citadel. The very short-stemmed Peer Gynt starts my picking season in October, Citadel is a little taller and, conveniently, at its best around Christmas. With these varieties I can

pick from the bottom upwards by stages over a number of weeks. To continue the season after Christmas I grow Bedford-Market Rearguard which gives me every chance of picking well into March.

Varieties
Bedford-Market Rearguard: a late variety which will give pickings into March. Medium-sized sprouts.
Bedford-Fillbasket: an old variety and a heavy cropper. Tall growing so staking is necessary. Produces sprouts in October and November.
Citadel: this F_1 hybrid gives uniform sprouts in December and January. Sprouts remain in good condition on the plant for quite a long time.
Peer Gynt: a dwarf F_1 hybrid. Produces sprouts in October. The best choice for a small garden.
Roodnef-Early Button: produces small, even-sized sprouts ideal for freezing. An early cropper.

Cabbage

Spring Cabbage

This crop is planted in the autumn and grows slowly through the winter which it is able to withstand with little ill effect. It matures in the spring when green vegetables are at a premium.

Sowing and planting
I sow my early cabbage in the seed bed at the beginning of August which is a little later than usual practice. I sprinkle a little bromophos in the drill first, just in case any cabbage root fly are about.

I plant out in October fairly closely, leaving only 45cm (18in) between plants and rows. By sowing at this later time and planting close

together I have every other cabbage to cut as fresh leafy greens in March, when supplies of cabbage are at their lowest.

Feeding
Spring cabbage is at its hardiest when growth is slow so I am careful not to stimulate growth early on. February or March is the time to give it a boost, which I do with a handful of Growmore fertiliser sprinkled in a circle around the plant a few inches away from the stem. The careful hoeing in of the fertiliser with the Dutch hoe breaks the soil surface and, by letting in air and moisture, is an encouragement to root action.

Varieties
April: medium-sized pointed cabbage which grows quickly.
Harbinger: this small cabbage has a marvellous flavour.
Offenham-Flower of Spring: stands longer in the field without cracking and is larger than the two mentioned above. However it matures later.

Summer Cabbage

This is sown in the spring, to grow quickly and mature in the summer. This means that it comes in when peas, beans and a host of other summer vegetables are around in plenty. This should be borne in mind when deciding what and how much to grow. It is certainly only worthwhile going for top quality in my opinion.

Sowing and planting
Early-sown summer cabbage needs slight heat for germination and protection at seedling stage. I sow May Star and June Star, both round-ball head types, in the greenhouse in February and prick the seedlings out as soon as they can be handled into 8-cm (3-in) pots of peat potting compost. I then harden them off in the cold frame.

They can then be planted out 60cm (2ft) apart in early April. They go on, as one might expect, to heart for cutting in May and June respectively. For a main summer crop sow outdoors in the seed bed in March or April. If the weather is dry first water the drill with a fine rose to encourage germination.

Pests
If the weather is dry and warm as well, it is wise to dust along the length of the row with derris dust just before the seedlings emerge. This is a good precaution against flea beetle which eats holes in leaves and stem possibly to the point of causing total plant loss. The incidence of flea beetle becomes severe enough for action to be taken when the spring-sown crop meets with warm dry conditions on emergence. Summer cabbages grow when the threat of cabbage root fly is at its worst, so in addition to the earlier routine precautions (see page 44), I water along the row with a dilute solution of gamma HCH a month after planting out.

Varieties
Greyhound: a quick-growing pointed cabbage. Can be sown in June or even July to provide cabbage for cutting in October.
Hispi: a fast-growing F_1 hybrid. This pointed cabbage can be planted closer than other varieties. Good quality but must be harvested quickly once it has reached maturity or it will crack.
June Star: this ball-headed F_1 hybrid is good for sowing early in the greenhouse. Stands well without cracking.
May Star: another ball-headed F_1 hybrid which matures early if started in the greenhouse.

Winter Cabbage

These are very hardy and easy to grow, they crop to cover the more difficult months from August to April. Savoys are easily recognised by their dark-green crinkled leaves.

Sowing and planting
Sow all of this group in the seed bed in March or April. Sow very thinly so that the seedlings have plenty of room and really sturdy plants are produced, fit to stand the worst of the winter weather. Variety determines the rate of maturing and therefore the cutting time, so a selection is needed to cover the given period.

Plant out winter cabbage in May or June at a minimum distance of 60cm (2ft) between plants and rows. Plant in to firm soil using a dibber and firm in each plant with the heel of the boot. Then water the plants in with a solution of gamma HCH as the usual precaution against cabbage root fly.

General care

When the plants have established themselves it is a good idea to lightly hoe in a little Growmore fertiliser around each plant.

In late summer be particularly watchful for cabbage-white butterflies. Caterpillars must be dealt with promptly by spraying with liquid derris or gamma HCH. These plants have to stand the winter and with caterpillar damage they will become more vulnerable.

Varieties

Best of All: a large-headed savoy for early cutting.

Christmas Drumhead: a good variety for, as its name suggests, cutting around Christmas time.

January King: late-maturing variety with a solid head. Can be cut in December but will stand until March or April.

Rearguard: a smaller variety, but will stand at maturity longer than most.

Selected Drumhead: medium sized drumhead cabbage maturing early.

Cauliflower

Of all the brassicas the cauliflower is the most difficult to grow to perfection. To produce a good cauliflower growth must go ahead without a check of any sort all the way from germination to maturity. Overcrowding or standing too long in the seed bed, becoming pot bound, suffering cold or drought after transplanting are all factors adversely affecting growth and liable to spoil the crop. Most noticeably this leads to 'buttoning', which is the formation of miniature curds instead of the normal sizeable ones. Although none are improved by a check most brassicas make some sort of recovery; this is not so with cauliflowers.

On the subject of varieties, most recent F_1 hybrid introductions have been bred with the commercial grower in mind. They are designed to give him uniform growth and maturity of the whole crop reached within a period of a week or so. This is ideal for minimum cost picking. From my own garden, though, I want a succession of cauliflowers reaching their peak individually over as long a time as possible. Therefore, I go back to the well-tried ordinary varieties, such as All the Year Round. They are reliable and not so dependant on exact sowing and transplanting dates.

Summer cauliflower

For my first summer cauliflowers I begin in February or March. I sow very thinly in a pan of peat seed-sowing compost and germinate in the greenhouse propagating frame at approximately 13°C (55°F). I take the pan out of the propagating frame as soon as the seedlings break the surface, otherwise they would become drawn and weak. The variety Classic has proved just right for this sowing. The seedlings are pricked out singly into 8-cm (3-in) pots of peat potting compost and grown on in the quite cool conditions on the greenhouse bench. They are hardened off in the cold frame, ready for planting out under

Bend a few of the inner leaves over the curd of maincrop cauliflower to prevent it yellowing

cloches late March or early April.

The cauliflower has a greater attraction for the cabbage root fly than any other brassica. I bear this in mind right from the seedling stage by giving potted seedlings and rows of seedlings a watering with liquid HCH before planting out. This is as well as carrying out the routine planting out precautions described on page 44 as both transplanting and thinning out attract the fly.

Maincrop

For a maincrop I sow during March to May, very thinly in the seed bed. Then I plant out on firm ground spacing the plants 60cm (2ft) apart each way. I always choose the sturdiest of the slightly undersized plants in the seed bed for planting out, as they are the most likely ones to produce large curds. All lanky specimens should be discarded. As transplanting can impose the all-deciding growth check, anyone constantly having bad results is well advised to make direct sowings only. To do this sow three seeds at positions 60cm (2ft) apart in rows 60cm (2ft) apart and thin out as soon as possible, leaving the strongest seedling at each position.

A developing curd is protected by its leaves, but once it is exposed to sunlight the snowy-white curd begins to yellow. Once peak condition is reached break the leaves closest to the centre over the curd to delay yellowing if the cauliflower is not to be cut immediately for use.

Winter cauliflowers

These are sown in the usual way in April or May and planted out in June or July, again with 60cm (2ft) between rows and plants. They stand in the ground for almost twelve months so perhaps the space cannot always be afforded in the small vegetable garden. The winter varieties are the hardiest and they grow strong protecting leaves around the curd, even so the best crops are produced in mild areas and in less severe winters.

The curds are sensitive to severe frost and those maturing from January till March may need the protection of hessian sacks or such-like material overnight during hard spells of weather as well as bending over the leaves. A frosted curd is quite spoilt and of no culinary use.

Boron deficiency

The occurrence of hollow stems indicates a boron deficiency in the soil. No disease is involved although the affected stems do deteriorate more quickly. Act only after the symptoms have appeared and then very carefully apply borax at the rate of 25g per 28 sq m (1oz per 30 sq yd) and no more. At higher rates borax begins to act as a weedkiller. To simplify the spreading of so small a dosage mix the correct amount of borax with a quantity of fine dry sand and sprinkle this very evenly over the area.

Varieties
Summer cauliflower
All the Year Round: the variety I grow for a long cropping period. Fine large curds suitable for exhibition.
Autumn Giant-Veitch's Self Protecting: sow in May for autumn cropping. The inner leaves grow over the curd slightly to protect it from early frosts.
Classic: best for an early sowing under glass. Good curd of fine flavour.

Winter cauliflower
English Winter-Progress: very hardy so suitable for growing in the north. Sow in May to harvest in May the following year.
Walcheren Winter: Sow in May to harvest the following April. Rather less hardy than English Winter-Progress.

Kale is extremely hardy and withstands the severest of frosts during the winter, however, it does occupy the ground for a long time. It will crop well on the most exposed sites where other brassicas have failed.

I choose Tall Green Curled which is the typical curly kale. Besides being a very good winter vegetable it is also the decorative value of the plant which appeals to me; the dark green intricately-curled leaves are so attractive during the autumn.

Sowing and planting

Sow in the seed bed in April or May and transplant in June or July spacing plants 60cm (2ft) apart with 60cm (2ft) between rows.

Curly kale is an attractive hardy winter vegetable. **Inset:** Kohl rabi, variety Purple Vienna

However, I usually find that a short row of kale is sufficient, and will give an abundant crop of shoots for harvesting during the winter and spring.

Harvesting
Picking can start in late November but the flavour improves after frost. Begin picking at the growing point and then continue downwards taking only the young shoots as they appear, the older leaves soon become too strong in flavour. These large leafy plants can get untidy during their long growing season, so to keep them clean and healthy I remove all yellowing leaves as they occur and add them to the compost heap.

Kohl Rabi

The edible part of kohl rabi looks like a root vegetable but is in fact the swollen bulbous stem developed just about ground level. The flavour is a cross between turnip and cabbage. Although it is an acquired taste, the reason many people dislike it comes from letting the swollen stem become too large. Up to the size of a tennis ball it is mild and tender, after that it goes on to become strong, coarse and off putting.

Sowing and growing
It can be grown for succession by sowing short rows from April to June. Sow thinly in rows 45cm (18in) apart. Thin out plants to 38cm (15in) apart in the row as soon as possible. Kohl rabi is quick growing and reaches maturity in about twelve weeks.

Varieties
Purple Vienna: this variety has, in my experience, the best flavour and remains palatable when it is somewhat on the large side.

51

LEAVES & STALKS

Of all the leaf and stalk vegetables leeks are probably the most popular, although celery with its possibility of being used as a cooked vegetable, a crisp addition to the salad bowl or as a snack at a party, comes a very close second. The leaf vegetables such as spinach and the several types of leaf beets are still not all that widely used in this country but they certainly deserve to be more extensively grown. Rhubarb is classified as a vegetable but mainly served as a sweet although in other countries it is sometimes eaten as a vegetable. Apart from the celery and the leeks, all these leaf and stalk vegetables are only suitable for the table when young and tender, most of them are on the bitter side when grown to maturity.

Celery

As celery is a descendant of a bog-loving plant it is understandable that these plants have a great need of moisture. I still favour the old-fashioned way of growing celery in trenches. This is the most satisfying and the most successful, with soil conditions as near as possible to that of the plants' original habitat. One of the best areas for celery growing is Cambridgeshire with its highly-organic slowly-decaying peat content. But any ground can be prepared to such an extent that good celery growing is possible; be it clay, light loam or sandy soil.

Preparing the soil

To grow trench celery, open up a trench early in the year, about 30cm (12in) deep and 45cm (18in) wide. If the sub-soil is of poor quality take another 20cm (8in) out of the trench and replace this with well-rotted compost or manure. The sub-soil which has been removed can be left on the sides to weather during the winter and used for earthing up during the growing season. A further amount of well-rotted compost or manure is worked into the bottom of the trench to act as a moisture-holding sponge. The trench is then left exposed till planting time. For self-blanching celery these preparations are not necessary as this can be grown on the flat but it will still need a good, well-cultivated moisture-holding soil.

Sowing and planting

I sow during the second half of March using a seed-sowing compost. The seeds should be sown thinly and then lightly covered with compost. Water the pans or trays using a fine rose before placing the seeds in a propagating frame at a temperature of about 16°C (60°F). Germination will take about a fortnight.

At the stage of the first true leaves prick out the seedlings into a tray filled with peat potting compost, allowing 5cm (2in) between seedlings. Gradually harden the seedlings off and plant out into the trench 30cm (12in) apart early in June. If the weather is dry, water the plants thoroughly and make sure

Plant out young celery 30cm (12in) apart in a prepared trench. A quick crop of lettuce or radish can be grown on the ridges either side

Sowing and Harvesting Chart

Crop	When to sow in the open	When to sow under glass	When to plant out	Distance between plants	Distance between rows	When to harvest
Celery trench		March	June	30cm (12in)	1.2m (4ft)	October - February
self-blanching		March	June	23cm (9in)	23cm (9in)	August - October
Leeks	March	January	May	23cm (9in)	38cm (15in)	October - March
Spinach summer	March - July				30cm (12in)	June - September
winter	August				30cm (12in)	October - April
New Zealand	May - June			25cm (10in)	30cm (12in)	June - October
spinach beet	April or June - July			25cm (10in)	30cm (12in)	June - April
Swiss chard	April - July			25cm (10in)	45cm (18in)	July - September
Rhubarb			November or March	1m (3ft)		January - June

that the plants are never short of water. Celery suffers a growth check if it is ever short of moisture. To make optimum use of space, level the tops of the ridges on both sides of the

Earth up trench celery to blanch the stems as they grow. Avoid getting soil into the growing centres

trench and sow lettuce or radish on them as a catch crop while the celery is still young.

Blanching

When the plants are 25cm (10in) high, start earthing up after removing any side shoots at the bases of the plants. Earthing up excludes the light from the stems so that they become blanched. As the plants grow, earthing up is repeated at intervals but at no time should the growing centre of the plants be covered with soil as this could cause rotting. In my experience wrapping the plants up in newspaper or corrugated paper encourages slugs and therefore should only be done if this pest is not around. For exhibition celery it is better to put drainpipes round the plants to obtain long blanched stems.

Self-blanching celery

Self-blanching varieties are planted on the flat much closer together, 25cm (9in) each way, than the trench varieties. The closeness of the plants helps to blanch and lengthen the stalks without the need for earthing up.

Leeks are truly winter-hardy, standing up to the frost better than most vegetables

Pests and diseases

Celery fly larvae cause blisters in the leaves, an intensive attack can spoil a crop. Spray with gamma HCH or fenitrothion in June, repeat if and when blisters appear. Celery blight is a leaf spot disease and seed is now dressed with thiram to prevent it. Spray with a copper fungicide at the first sign of trouble.

Varieties
Trench
Giant Red: one of the hardiest varieties, if grown well will stand outside till January.
Giant Pink: the next hardy variety; of excellent quality for the table.
Giant White: this variety needs care to produce heads at their best. Is ready from October onwards and is one of the best for table quality.
Self-blanching
Golden Self-blanching: a very early variety which is ready in August.
American Green: an October variety. Both of these lack the crispness of the traditional trench grown varieties.

Leeks

The leek is one of the most important winter vegetables, at full maturity it is able to stand very low temperatures without losing any of its flavour and without being damaged to any extent. Leeks can be grown anywhere in this country and often do better in the colder parts than in the south.

Preparing the soil

Leeks, being a member of the onion family, do like to have their roots into good fertile soil with some moisture-holding capacity. I prepare a bed for leeks with as much care as an onion bed and with as good a foundation of well-rotted compost or manure, working in a balanced fertiliser such as fish, blood and bone in the final preparation. A deep planting tilth is useful so that earthing up later on does not prove too difficult.

Sowing and planting

For good results a long growing season is needed and to achieve this I sow my leeks in boxes in the greenhouse in January. After germination, which takes place with ease at a temperature of 13°C (55°F), I prick the seedlings out as soon as they are large enough to handle. If I want exhibition leeks I put them into 8-cm (3-in) pots, otherwise into seed trays with the seedlings spaced 5cm (2in) apart each way. Gradually they are hardened off in the cold frame and eventually planted out in mid-May.

My second sowing of leeks is in the seed bed in March. Germination is rather slow outside and it sometimes helps to cover the seed with cloches till germination takes place. Sow very thinly as leeks do not like to be overcrowded. Make sure that there is no weed competition in the seed bed and if weeds do appear, carefully remove them by hand so that the slowly-growing seedlings are not disturbed or uprooted.

For planting out I use a dibber to make the planting hole, then drop the small leek plant carefully in the hole and slowly dribble in a little water so that the roots of the plantlet are well covered with damp soil. I plant my leeks about 23cm (9in) apart with 38cm (15in) between rows.

General care
Leeks are not very demanding provided the pre-planting preparations have been well done, if given too much nitrogenous fertiliser the leaves become rather soft and the keeping qualities are not so good. The only time when I apply a fertiliser during the growing season is when the plants appear to stop growing. I then use a balanced liquid fertiliser, for at this time quick action is necessary and water is as important to the leeks as feeding.

I start earthing up when the plants are approximately 45cm (18in) high. During the growing season keep progressively earthing up to produce a long length of blanched stem before the winter. Leeks are lifted as required but if the land is needed to prepare for other crops during the winter, they can be lifted and heeled in in some convenient spot.

Pests and diseases
Most diseases in leeks can be avoided by maintaining a strict crop rotation discipline but if white rot infects the ground no leeks or any other member of the onion family should be grown on that spot for several years. Other fungus diseases can be controlled by spraying with a liquid copper fungicide. In the event of an attack of leek moth caterpillars, spray with derris.

Varieties
For exhibitions
Mammoth: a really large leek of fine quality if grown with care.
Prizetaker: this will make a splendid plant if well grown.
For table use
Musselburgh: more winter-hardy than most varieties. An old and popular variety.
Royal Favourite: excellent flavour and quality.

Spinach

Spinach of any kind is grown for its leaves only and should be picked when very young and tender otherwise the flavour becomes extremely strong and unpleasant.

Both the leaves and the midribs of seakale beet can be eaten, each as a separate vegetable

Summer Spinach

This can be grown as a catch crop between rows of slower-growing vegetables as it matures quickly and very soon bolts to seed. The best soil for growing spinach is a well-dug medium to heavy loam but a lighter soil with some well-rotted compost or manure worked in is also suitable.

When preparing the soil take in 60 to 100g per m (2 to 3oz per sq yd) of a balanced fertiliser such as Growmore just before sowing. The earliest sowing of summer spinach can be made in March and then for succession sow at fortnightly intervals until the end of July. Sow the seed in shallow drills 30cm (12in) apart. No thinning out is needed as it should be cut at frequent intervals.

This type of spinach runs to seed very rapidly especially when grown on a light, hot, sandy soil.

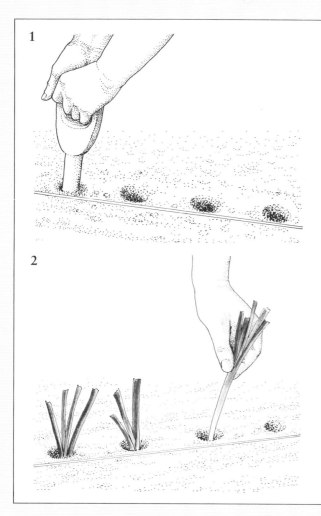

Planting out leeks
1 Make planting holes 23cm (9in) apart with a dibber
2 Drop one leek plant into each hole
3 Dribble water in to wash soil over plant roots. There is no need for further filling in as this will happen naturally in time

Winter Spinach

This is grown in the same way as summer spinach. However it is sown during August and will crop from October or November until April. Aphids are the only pests, apart from slugs, which attack spinach. Control by regular spraying with malathion or derris. Wet conditions and overcrowding encourage downy mildew, if this attacks the foliage spray with a fungicide based on zineb.

New Zealand Spinach

This is not a true spinach but a 'cut and come again' leafy vegetable with a similar flavour. It

New Zealand Spinach

does not bolt as quickly as summer spinach and certainly stands better in hot dry weather. Sowings can be made from May onwards to July in open ground, but the seedlings should be thinned out to 25cm (10in) apart. The leaves can be picked regularly from mid-June onwards and plants will crop till the first frost.

Spinach Beet

This is also known as perpetual spinach and is another 'cut and come again' vegetable. The soil and cultural requirements are similar to those for summer spinach. Sow during April in shallow drills and thin out to 25cm (10in) apart. It withstands dry periods better than the other types of spinach described here. It is winter hardy when sown in late June or early July and will provide a valuable early spring crop.

Swiss Chard

This is another name for seakale beet, not to be confused with seakale which is a completely different vegetable. Swiss chard has broad spinach-like leaves and large white petioles. They should be cooked as separate vegetables; the leaves as spinach and the petioles as asparagus — both make a very good dish.

Sow from April onwards till July in shallow drills 45cm (18in) apart. Thin out as soon as possible to 25cm (10in) apart. Cultivation is the same as for summer spinach. Swiss chard runs to seed if the conditions are dry and warm, but later sowings would stand a better chance to grow to maturity in the autumn.

Rhubarb

Once established a rhubarb plant will crop regularly for many years, requiring very little attention for the returns it gives. It prefers a sunny open site that has been well dug and had plenty of well-rotted manure or compost incorporated into it. The crowns should be planted in November or March, spacing the plants 1m (3ft) apart.

Pulling the stalks

No stalks should be pulled during the first year after planting. This is to enable the crown to become strong and produce good buds. During the second season after planting some stalks can be pulled, but don't overdo it. After this the plant can be cropped normally.

General care

Any seed heads that appear should be cut off. The plants benefit greatly from an annual mulch of well-rotted compost or manure. This should be applied in the early spring, first ensuring the soil is moist.

Forcing indoors

Roots should be lifted in November or December and left on the soil exposed to the frost for a week or so. For best results the roots should be about three years old, but old roots can be cut into several pieces. Each piece will grow as long as it has at least one fat bud.

They don't require much space and can be put under the greenhouse bench or in boxes, with a little soil between the roots. This should be kept moist at all times. Once growth begins the temperature should be raised to about 12°C (53°F) and the plants can be forced in darkness. They will be ready for pulling in about six weeks.

Forcing outside

The rhubarb patch can be severely depleted by lifting the roots and forcing indoors, as afterwards the crowns are of no further use. An alternative is to cover the crown *in situ* with a box or barrel, or even a dustbin provided it is open at both ends. The container must be high enough to allow the rhubarb sticks to grow up without emerging into daylight.

Put some wisps of straw inside to reduce the light intensity and to draw the rhubarb up towards the stronger light. This process takes longer than forcing indoors but you will still have an established plant capable of cropping.

Varieties

Champagne: a variety difficult to beat for quality. Suitable for forcing outdoors.
Timperley Early: best variety for lifting and forcing indoors. Fine quality.

57

MARROWS

Marrows, courgettes, pumpkins and squashes are all members of the same family. Although marrows are still a popular vegetable in this country, the general trend is going more and more towards courgettes. These, after all, are only very young marrows, cut when the fruit is approximately 15cm (6in) long and the flavour so very much better. Giant marrow and pumpkin competitions used to be popular but when the fruit reaches that size it is virtually inedible. For winter storage marrows and their relations are best when they are only of moderate size.

Squashes are less watery than marrows and are becoming more popular in this country. Their fruits, as with marrows, come in different shapes and colours. Pumpkins have thicker skins and more dry matter than any other members of this family and are truly delicious when cooked properly.

Sowing
I sow the seeds of this family on edge, singly in 8-cm (3-in) pots filled with a peat seed compost, in the middle of April and place the pots in a progagating frame kept at a

Marrows come in all shapes and sizes like the large round variety Tender and True. Others, like Green Bush and Golden Zucchini, can be cut young as courgettes or allowed to grow into larger fruits with no subsequent deterioration in quality

temperature of 16 to 18.5°C (60 to 65°F). Germination takes place in a few days. Then when the seedlings are about 5cm (2in) high they are placed on the greenhouse bench at a temperature of about 10 to 13°C (50 to 55°F) and later hardened off in the cold frame at the beginning of May. The plants can be planted out under cloches from the second week in May onwards or without protection from the end of May to beginning of June.

Planting

There is no better medium for growing these vegetables than well-rotted compost. In a small garden they can be grown on top of the compost heap but if there is sufficient space it is a good alternative to plant them in the vegetable plot. Make a hole for each plant spacing them 60cm (2ft) apart. Fill each hole with well-rotted compost to a depth of about 45cm (18in). Leave a small saucer-like hollow around each plant. This will make watering effective and help to conserve the moisture where it is most needed.

Care and cultivation

Right from the start it is very important to keep the soil moisture-level high, as marrows always need a continuous supply of moisture in the ground. From July onwards I apply a liquid fertiliser at fortnightly intervals, this helps to keep the plants producing fruit. This is especially important for courgettes as they are required to continuously supply young fruits. Marrows may be left on the plant till about the middle of September when they can then be harvested for storage during the early part of the winter. Store them by keeping them in nets hanging from hooks in a frost-free airy place.

Pests and diseases

There are no major disease problems when marrows and their relatives are grown outside, they are, however, liable to be attacked by slugs and aphids. If the weather is inclined to be wet at planting time I put a few protected slug pellets near to the plants. If the need does arise to spray for aphid control, check the directions and precautions on the insecticide label, for all marrows and related plants are susceptible to certain chemicals.

Varieties

I no longer grow the trailing varieties as these take up too much room, the new bush type varieties are certainly more suitable for the smaller gardens.
Tender and True: my favourite marrow. It is round, medium sized and has real quality but is one of the varieties less suitable for growing as courgettes.
Golden Zucchini: a golden-fruited variety suitable for growing as courgettes. The fruit, even when cut a little on the large side, is still of excellent quality and flavour.
Green Bush: dark-green fruit suitable for growing as courgettes. Excellent quality and flavour even when cut a little on the large size.
Long Green: good-keeping marrow for early winter use. A trailing variety.
Long White: a pure white trailing variety. Good-keeping marrow for early winter use.

Pumpkins

Hundredweight and Mammoth: these are the varieties I grow. They each grow to an enormous size and will try to achieve their descriptive names.

Squashes

Table Queen Bush: an American bush variety of squash, many of the other squashes are trailing varieties but all of them are good keepers and can be used as an addition to the winter diet, store as the marrows.

LUXURY CROPS

Luxury vegetables to me are those which cannot be classed as necessary but which, with a little expertise and the expenditure of somewhat more time, space and patience than usual, add greatly to the enjoyment of home growing. In my opinion, to be a practical proposition growing luxuries must not be too demanding on resources such as heating and protection, and there must be a good prospect of success from the start. Taking into account the British climate with its comparatively short summer season and choosing the right varieties I am still left with quite a lot of scope for luxury.

Globe Artichokes

When one considers that the edible part of the globe artichoke consists only of the fleshy scales surrounding the unopened flower heads, it is obvious that the ratio of usable crop to occupied growing space is the deciding factor. If space is no problem the rest is easy.

Most soils are suitable, the preference being for those on the lighter side. Dig the soil well before planting, working in plenty of well-rotted manure or compost. The plant is moisture loving and therefore the soil must have a good moisture-holding capacity if the heads are to reach their full size. Another must is sunshine, so choose an open sunny site.

Planting

Globe artichokes can be grown from seed but I do not recommend it, there is a lot of variation among seedlings and the essential culling of poor specimens at an advanced stage takes quite a toll. The best way of propagating is to take suckers from established plants in March or April. Remove them cleanly from close to the main stem with some root attached using a sharp knife. Pot the suckers individually in 13-cm (5-in) pots

Sowing and Harvesting Chart

Crop	When to sow in the open	When to sow under glass	When to plant out	Distance between plants	Distance between rows	When to harvest
Globe artichokes			March - April	60cm (2ft)	1m (3ft)	July - October
Asparagus	April		April	38cm (15in)	45cm (18in)	April - June 21st
Aubergines		February - March				July - September
Peppers		March - April	June	45cm (18in)		July - September
Sweet corn	May	April	May	30cm (12in)	30cm (12in)	August - September

61

of peat potting compost. As soon as a good root system has developed plant out in rows 1m (3ft) apart with 60cm (2ft) between plants.

Head production

There are only one or two heads on each plant in the first season, but then three or four seasons follow in which there are five or six good heads to be cut from each plant. I remove the heads forming on the side shoots to increase the size of heads on the main stem. From four or five years old onwards fewer and smaller heads are produced so it is best to anticipate the need for replanting every four or five years by taking suckers from existing plants.

Water well during dry spells. Wait for the

Globe artichokes should be cut before the heads open

fleshy heads to mature between July and October but cut them before they open; for once the scales have opened the heads are inedible. After cropping I cut the artichokes right down and tidy up the row. The plants are hardy but it is advisable to give them some protection during a severe winter by putting some dry straw or bracken over the crowns.

Varieties

Gros Vert de Laon: excellent variety producing large heads of good flavour.

Asparagus

With its few health problems asparagus is an easy crop to grow if you start with clean land, keep it that way and are not in a hurry. For the commercial grower the preparation work and constant weeding are expensive, but for the amateur gardener there is the opportunity to provide the expensive element himself and then enjoy an otherwise extravagant vegetable. Once established, the upkeep of an asparagus bed is routine.

Raising from seed

Plants can be raised from seed but the waiting time is long from sowing to cutting the first crop. Sow in April in a well-prepared weed-free seed bed, sowing thinly in a drill 1cm (½in) deep. Thin out the seedlings to 15cm (6in) apart and make sure they grow without any weed competition.

They will have made sizeable crowns by the following April. They can then be transplanted to the permanent bed or left in the seedling row for a further year. This would give an opportunity for the female seed-bearing plants to be identified and discarded before the final planting. In a permanent bed planted with all male crowns there will not be the tediously continuous job of weeding out unwanted seedlings.

The more usual way to start is by purchasing one-, two- or three-year-old crowns for planting in mid-April. I choose one-year-old crowns, they settle down quickly after planting and are generally cheaper. The older crowns offer no advantage from a time point of view for whatever the age the crowns are at planting time, cutting must not begin until the third season after planting. A massive root system has to be built up before the crown is ready to take the strain of cutting. Heavy cropping depends on the slow build-up of crown size over a number of well-managed years.

Opposite: Asparagus, variety Conover's Colossal

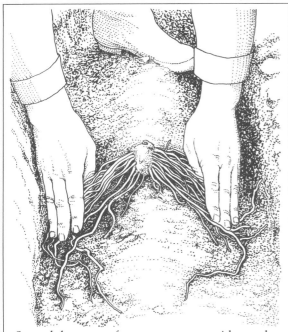

Spread the roots of asparagus over a ridge at the bottom of a trench. Cover the crowns quickly to ensure they do not dry out

Preparing the site

Asparagus is no match for perennial weeds. If the perennial-weed problem is great it is wise to delay planting for a year and to sort the problem out. As a preliminary get rid of all roots of bindweed, couch grass, dock, nettle, thistle and similar weeds. If there are slugs around deal with them in advance by the use of slug baits and cleaning up of their breeding places.

A wide range of soils can be made satisfactory if drainage is good, waterlogging destroys crowns and any survivors only make poor growth. A deep rich medium soil is best but it must be alkaline. Where the pH is below 6.5 an annual dressing of hydrated lime is to be applied. It is not a good idea to replant an old asparagus bed, choose a new position in full sun and as protected from strong winds as possible. Wind can blow the fern about in the summer and healthy undamaged fern growth is an essential part of the asparagus year.

Where there is little space to spare a single

row of crowns is certainly worthwhile. My bed, which supplies the family and more besides, is 1.2m (4ft) wide, 6m (20ft) long and planted with three rows of crowns 38cm (15in) apart each way.

Prepare the area of the new bed as early as possible in the autumn. Dig deeply, breaking up the bottom to provide an easy root run below the first spit. Work in plenty of well-rotted compost or manure and in early March, prior to planting, apply a dressing of hydrated lime on all but chalky soils. Mid-April is the ideal planting time, so order crowns well in advance specifying the time of delivery.

Planting

Choose the first day after delivery when the air is damp for planting. For the young roots are fleshy and, therefore, liable to dehydrate quickly, and this is often the cause of later plant failure. Leave the parcel unopened until planting is begun and then cover the bulk of the crowns with a damp sack as you go along. For planting each row dig out a trench 25cm (10in) deep and 30cm (12in) wide. Make a sloping ridge in the bottom for the crowns to be placed on 38cm (15in) apart, with their roots sloping downwards either side. Cover them quickly and carefully with fine soil.

Weeding

From the start do not let any annual weeds establish or seed themselves. Cutting of the spears can begin in the third season after planting; in subsequent years the percentage of thick quality spears will increase. While the bed is clear the surface can be kept weed-free by gentle shallow hoeing but once spears appear at the end of April, hand weeding is best. Chemical weedkillers are used on established beds but I prefer hand weeding, it is a small job if done at each cutting time and there are no risks.

Cutting

Go over the bed every two or three days cutting all spears that are 8cm (3in) above the surface. Their thickness may vary but all should be cut to keep up the maximum cropping capacity. Use either the traditional asparagus knife, as I do, or a suitable long-bladed sharp knife. Go down beside the bud

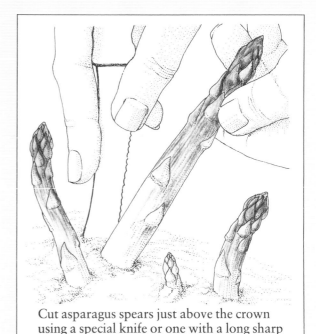

Cut asparagus spears just above the crown using a special knife or one with a long sharp blade

stem cutting it off above the crown, trying not to damage either the crown or young buds. Careless cutting adversely affects the yield.

If the bed is to maintain its cropping capacity over a number of years the crowns must have sufficient time each year to build up their food reserves before the end of the growing season. For this reason I insist on no more cutting after 21st June. It is hard to see all those succulent spears apparently going to waste but from then on the fern is vital to the build up of the crown for next season. Without the renewal of strength afforded by its growth the bed will deteriorate.

General care

By the end of October the fern will have turned yellow indicating that its work is done. Only then should the fern be cut down to ground level. Do any weeding necessary and apply a dressing of well-rotted compost or manure topped with a layer of soil from the sides of the bed, being careful not to disturb the wide-ranging root system. I burn the fern as I find it too woody for the compost heap.

To ensure that the bed has enough nutrients to supply spears for cutting and for building up the crowns' strength for the next season, I give two applications of fertiliser. The first is made in February or early March and the second one when cutting has stopped on the 21st June. In both instances I apply a balanced general fertiliser at the rate of 100 to 120g per sq m (3 to 4oz per sq yd). In the case of a young uncropped bed with its fern already at full height in June a liquid fertiliser feed or an application of an organic fertiliser is best as they do not incur any risk of foliage scorch.

I cannot resist being enthusiastic at length over asparagus as it rewards the gardener so consistently for so long, maybe forty years and more, for just his stock-in-trade care and patience.

Varieties
Connover's Colossal: a popular old variety.
Regal: this is my choice for quality. Raised in this country.

Aubergines

The aubergine or egg plant must have sunshine and warmth, it is a semi-tropical plant and with its strong dark stems, purple flowers and glossy purple fruit adds an exotic

Above: Allow some peppers to turn red on the plant at the end of the season
Below left: Aubergines crop well given protection

touch to the greenhouse. In exceptionally sunny summers growing outside can be successful but I always complete my growing season in the greenhouse.

Sowing and planting
I sow in February in a pan of peat seed-sowing compost and germinate in the propagating frame at 18.5°C (65°F). While they are still small I prick out the seedlings into 8-cm (3-in) pots and then, before there is any risk of the plants becoming potbound I pot on into 20-cm (8-in) pots of peat potting compost. Plants can make do with 15- or 18-cm (6- or 7-in) pots but those in larger pots or growing bags will outcrop them.

General care
Growing bags are a good alternative but I prefer my aubergines in pots on the bench where I can watch them more easily and deal at the first sign with the usual constant aphid problem. Aubergines have the same attraction for aphids as do peppers. I spray on sight with malathion or a quassia and rotonone mixture, this will also deal with any occurrence of red spider mite.

65

I pinch out the growing tip when the plants are about 15 cm (6 in) tall, to make them bushy and so ensure that there are plenty of laterals for producing fruit. At an early stage I give a cane for support and loosely tie in the laterals, as once the fruits have formed they soon become quite weighty.

Aubergines must never dry out if the fleshy fruits are to mature in top condition and also because dryness at the roots encourages red spider mite. From the time the first fruits develop I give a weekly feed with a high-potash liquid fertiliser at the strength recommended for tomatoes. Feeding and careful watering will keep the cropping going.

Varieties
Early Long Purple: an old favourite variety.
Moneymaker: an early cropping F_1 hybrid.

Attempts to grow this crop outside are being made in this country but success is usually limited to the favoured south.

Sowing and planting
I grow my peppers in the greenhouse or under cloches, sowing the seed in a pan of peat seed-sowing compost in March. Germination takes place in the propagating frame kept at 16 to 18.5°C (60 to 65°F). From a mid-April sowing, germination can be successful on the kitchen windowsill. Cover the seed pan with plastic film to prevent the seed from drying out and move the seedlings to the greenhouse as soon as possible.

My seedlings are pricked out singly into 8-cm (3-in) pots for growing on the greenhouse bench, with the temperature kept at 10°C (50°F). In May they are planted either into 20-cm (8-in) pots of peat potting compost or into peat growing bags, two to a bag, and grown on for cropping in the cold greenhouse. For growing under cloches I do not plant outside till early June when frost is no danger.

Care and cultivation
Peppers need the same conditions as tomatoes but not such constant attention for training. If there is no set back the plants become bushy

naturally but if they are allowed to get potbound or dried out they are liable to run up a single stem. If this happens pinch out the growing tip to induce the production of side shoots. In all plants thin out weak lateral growths to prevent overcrowding which is the common cause of undersized fruits.

Once fruit has begun to set, I give a weekly feed with a high-potash liquid tomato fertiliser at a third of the rate recommended for tomatoes. If need be, I give the plants a cane to support them but this depends on the variety. Shortage of water will cause a kind of blossom end rot similar to that in tomatoes, so for perfect fruit the plants must never be short of water. Unripe fruits are picked as green peppers and picking at that stage ensures a long season of continuous fruit production. As the season goes on I usually leave a few fruits to ripen and become red.

Pests and diseases
Peppers attract a plant-louse type of aphid which can multiply at an alarming rate and completely debilitate the pepper plant. Watch for it on the undersides of the leaves and spray with malathion on sight, a weekly spray with quassia and rotonone will also keep the plants clean.

Varieties
New Ace: this F_1 hybrid has been my most successful variety. It crops early.
Outdoor: suitable for growing under cloches in the south of the country.

Sweet Corn

Sweetcorn loves the sun and a long summer season in which to ripen its cobs. Our summer stops rather short for the older slower-maturing varieties but the introduction of early-maturing hybrids has meant that cropping results, at least in the southern half of the country, can be consistently reliable. I find that First of All and Earliest ripen well within the length of season we get in the Midlands.

The soil should be deep and well prepared but not too richly manured or else leaf growth will be luxuriant at the expense of cob production. Choose the sunniest site on your plot.

Sowing and planting

To get an early start sow in the cold greenhouse in mid-April (the greenhouse only needs to be heated slightly during cold nights). I put single seeds 2.5 cm (1 in) deep in small peat pots filled with peat potting compost. In this compost the seedlings form a large ball of roots quickly. They are then planted outside under cloches in mid-May.

Sweetcorn is sensitive to frost so cloche protection is necessary until all danger of frost has gone. It is important not to let the plants become pot bound or stay too long in seed boxes. To have a good chance of maturity by the end of the summer the plants must go out while they are growing rapidly. They will maintain the growth rate and also tiller well with the prospect of a maximum number of cobs per plant.

An early variety sown direct in a really sunny spot in mid-May should prove satisfactory. I plant out in a square with plants 30 cm (12 in) apart each way, never in single or double rows. When planted in a square the plants give each other support and pollination is infinitely better.

Care and cultivation

First of All and Earliest are relatively short varieties, growing to about 1 m (just over 3 ft) and need no extra support. For taller varieties

Always plant sweet corn in blocks to ensure cross pollination

Ripe sweet corn ready to harvest

I would put a stake at each corner of the block and take a couple of strong strings around.

There are male and female flowers on each sweetcorn plant and cob production depends on efficient pollination. Pollen from the male flowers on top of the plant must fall onto the female tassel-like flowers lower down. The cobs are already forming within their tight sheath of leaves but the grains inside will only swell evenly if pollination is good. Undeveloped grains showing up here and there and particularly at the top of the cob at harvest time are evidence of poor pollination. Water generously during dry spells to keep the cobs succulent.

Ripening

As the cobs are closely wrapped with leaves it is not easy to tell when to harvest. I do a bit of unwrapping on the plant and test a few grains with my thumb nail, they are just right when the milky fluid inside is no longer clear but will coagulate. If the cobs are left beyond that stage the grains become mealy, then inedible.

Varieties

Earliest: short growing early variety.
First of All: can be ready in August if started off in April in the greenhouse.

HERBS

As with all plants herbs do best in a well prepared soil. So when starting a small plot for growing culinary herbs it is advisable to dig the ground over and incorporate some well-rotted compost into the soil. The main function of the compost will be to hold the moisture. For convenience it is a help to have the herbs growing as near to the kitchen as it is practicable but it is certainly not a necessity. Herbs like to be protected from the north and the east and the right position is more important than them being close at hand.

Herbs can be grown in the flower garden as well as in the vegetable garden and all of those mentioned in this chapter do well in pots or tubs. If grown in containers it is imperative to make sure that watering is adequate but not overdone, as waterlogging will kill the roots. Wherever herbs are grown they do like a sunny position and some protection from the frost. There is a wide range of culinary herbs but I have only included the mose useful ones.

Chives

This is a perennial plant and the smallest member of the onion family. It is very hardy and will produce its leaves throughout the year provided it is given the protection of a cloche during the winter months. It forms clumps and these can be divided in the spring and replanted 15cm (6in) apart. It can easily be grown from seed. When large enough to handle the young seedlings can be planted out 15cm (6in) apart. It is best to remove the flowers to encourage leaf development. Cut the leaves when they are young.

Garlic

Another member of the onion family, but this one is biennial. It is grown each year from a fresh clove of garlic (a segment of the bulb). Plant the clove into the soil with the pointed end just above ground level in February. When the foliage has died down, around July or August, the bulbs are ready for harvesting and drying.

Mint

Spearmint is the most common form, but peppermint and apple mint can also be grown, the latter probably having the best flavour. It is a very invasive plant and the best way of keeping it in check is to grow it either in a container or start a new plant with a freshly-dug piece of root. Dig up all the old roots in early spring and then some of the young root can be planted straight away in a container and forced for early use. Pick leaves young both for using fresh and for drying.

Parsley

This biennial member of the carrot family should be grown as an annual from seed. Sow the seed early in March or April, preferably indoors. Germination can take five or six weeks. Prick out the seedlings and later plant outside 15 to 20cm (6 to 8in) apart. Prevent attacks of carrot fly by sprinkling some bromophos in the planting holes. Always keep the young plants weed free and moist and remove flower stems when they appear. The leaves should be picked when they are young for the best flavour.

Sage

This is a woody perennial plant. The most common variety has grey-green leaves but there are other varieties with either purple or yellow leaves. Leaves must be picked young both for drying and for fresh use. The plant will become straggly after several years, when this happens it is best to propagate from heeled cuttings in late spring. Alternatively peg down branches and let them root during the growing season (this is known as layering). Sage grown from seed tends to produce a free-flowering plant.

Thyme

This is a small evergreen shrub which needs some protection in severe winters. As with sage the plant tends to become straggly after a few years but it will propagate itself from branches lying on the ground, these root spontaneously. Leaves are picked during the growing season. Do not pick leaves during the winter months unless the plant is grown under cover. In addition to the common thyme, lemon thyme is often preferred for its additional fragrance.

From left to right: Chives, spearmint, garlic, thyme, parsley and sage

Pests and Diseases

Pest	Damage	Plants Affected	Treatment
Aphids	There are several species of aphids attacking a number of vegetables. They suck sap from the leaves causing distortion and loss of vigour. They also spread virus disease in lettuce and potatoes.	Lettuce, beans, peas, potatoes and other vegetables	Spray with malathion and repeat when necessary. Always spray in the evening when the bees are resting.
Cabbage aphid	Mealy grey aphids attack leaves and shoots.	All brassicas, especially cabbages and Brussels sprouts	Spray with malathion or liquid derris mixed with a little washing-up liquid so the leaves and aphids are effectively wetted.
Cabbage root fly	White larvae feed on roots, eventually killing the plant.	All brassicas, especially serious on cauliflowers	Apply bromophos to planting hole and water with gamma HCH.
Cabbage white butterfly	Caterpillars eat leaves to skeletons, ruining the crop.	All brassicas, especially cabbages	Spray with derris or fenitrothion on sight. Add a little washing-up liquid to ensure wetting of foliage.
Carrot fly	The larvae attack the roots causing stunting and making the root unusable.	Carrot, parsley	Apply bromophos to the open seed drill. Water rows of seedlings with gamma HCH. Sow thinly to avoid thinning out but if this is necessary do this in the evening and apply bromophos afterwards.
Celery fly	The larvae feed on the leaves causing large blisters which check the growth of the plant. Attacks occur between May and October.	Celery, celeriac	Spray with HCH or fenitrothian in June. Repeat if blisters appear.
Lettuce root aphid	This aphid feeds on the roots causing yellowing and stunting of the growth and eventually the plant's death. It overwinters on Lombardy poplars. June and July are the critical months.	Lettuce	Water affected young plants with malathion or diazinon. Re-sow on fresh ground after watering the drill with either chemical.
Onion fly	The maggots feed on the roots causing serious damage, especially on direct sown crops.	Onion and related crops	Apply bromophos to the open drill before sowing. Water young seedling with HCH. Onion sets are rarely attacked.
Pea moth	The maggots are found in the pod eating the peas. Worst hit are crops that flower in June to August.	Peas	Spray with fenitrothion in the late evening when flowering commences. Repeat in two weeks.
Potato cyst eelworm	Cysts are carried on seed potatoes grown on infected soil. Infected plants die off early and fail to crop.	Potatoes	Wash seed potatoes. Keep to a strict crop rotation plan, applying organic matter to the soil. Plant certified seed. An expensive solution is to sterilize infected soil with dazomet. Do not plant on infected ground.

Pest	Damage	Plants Affected	Treatment
Red spider mite	Mites suck sap from leaves causing damage to foliage and a serious loss of vigour to plant.	Cucumber and tomatoes, especially if grown under glass	Keep humidity up in greenhouse by damping down. Keep plant roots moist. Spray plants with dimethoate or use azobenzene smokes. Clean greenhouse thoroughly every year.
Slugs and snails	Chew foliage.	Most young plants	Place slug baits or pellets under cover of a box with an entrance provided.
Whitefly	All stage feed on the leaves and excrete honeydew (a sticky solution that gums up the leaves and attracts moulds).	Tomatoes, especially in the greenhouse	Spray with malathion or resmethrin twice a week. Use lindane smokes fairly frequently.
Other pests	These can attack leaves, stems and roots.	Any plant	Spray with HCH.

Disease	Damage	Plants Affected	Treatment
Botrytis (grey mould)	A grey rot affects the leaves. Worst in cool damp conditions.	Lettuce, especially on overwintering crops	Remove infected leaves and clear away any plant debris. Raise the temperature in the greenhouse and only water plants when absolutely necessary.
Celery leaf spot	Black spots on foliage spread quickly in cool damp weather.	Celery, celeriac	Seed is now treated with thiram. At first sign of trouble spray with a copper fungicide.
Clubroot	Roots swell and decay causing plants to wilt and die. It can live in the soil for many years.	All brassicas	Apply 4% calomel dust to the seed bed before sowing and to the planting hole. Applying garden lime to the soil discourages the disease. Raise your own plants.
Damping off	Seedlings collapse and die after germination.	Seedlings under glass, especially tomatoes	Use sterilized seed composts. Water seedlings with a liquid copper fungicide.
Leaf mould	Pale grey patches appear on the undersides of the leaves, eventually becoming a thick brown felt. Reduces plant vigour and cropping.	Tomatoes, especially in the greenhouse	Spray with benomyl and repeat after two weeks. Improve circulation of air in the greenhouse.
Powdery mildew	Whitish patches develop on the leaves which eventually die.	Cucumbers grown under glass	On first sight spray with dinocap or use a dinocap smoke. Keep area around greenhouse weed free.
Wilt diseases	Plants collapse and die.	Cucumbers and tomatoes	Replace or sterilise the soil, using dazomet, before replanting. Use peat growing bags.
Virus	Spread by sucking insects such as aphids. Foliage becomes mottled, distorted or curled.	Lettuces, potatoes, cucumbers, tomatoes	Control sucking insects by spraying. For potatoes, plant certified seed bought from a reliable source.

FRUIT

At one time fruit growing in home gardens was seldom planned; gardeners either inherited old fruit trees of great height, planted varieties of their choice on unknown rootstocks or started hopefully by sowing pips. In nearly every case the trees grew so large that long ladders were needed at harvesting time, when maggoty and scabby fruit was the reward for the risks involved. Even if at that time insecticides and fungicides had been available it would have been almost impossible to apply them effectively as the fruit bearing branches were usually beyond the range of spraying equipment.

Research undertaken on behalf of the commercial fruit grower has changed all this. No longer does the modern gardener need a ladder for fruit picking and safe insecticides and fungicides are available to control the fruit pests and diseases with the minimum of effort. So quality fruit growing at home is now a worthwhile proposition.

In addition the increased knowledge on plant nutrition means that the gardener can achieve high yields of quality fruit and that he is in a far better position than the commercial grower when it comes to choice of varieties. Many of the finest-flavoured fruits suffer from transit and storage problems such as bruising and short shelf-life. Consequently they are not now grown commercially in any quantity. Whereas for the gardener, the superior qualities are far more rewarding when the distance and time between picking and eating is minimal.

With tree fruits it is important not only to choose varieties known to succeed in your district but to make sure that the rootstock on which they are budded or grafted is right for the way in which you wish to grow the trees. This will also determine the eventual size of the tree.

Pollination

Whilst a few varieties of apples, pears and plums are self-fertile, in other words will produce a crop without having a different variety as a near neighbour for cross pollination, most varieties do require at least one other compatible variety close at hand. Fertilisation of the open blossom is done by bees and insects which carry the pollen from one variety to the other. However both varieties must reach the open-blossom stage at the same time and, equally important, the temperature during the blossom period must be reasonably warm at some time during the hours of daylight for otherwise the pollen is not viable.

In addition to the part played by bees and pollinating insects, the wind is a contributary factor and should not be discounted. In periods of windy, dry, warm weather pollen grains are air borne over considerable distances. In small gardens knowledge of the neighbours' varieties can be very helpful as the bees, insects and wind are not inhibited by fences or hedges. However, whenever possible it is preferable to have the pollinators in your garden; neighbours have been known to fell the trees that were essential pollinators.

No such problems have to be considered in soft-fruit growing. Strawberries, raspberries and gooseberries only need the right weather conditions and the assistance of the bees and insects at blossom time for a good set of fruit.

Situation

Whilst it is not possible to alter the basic growing conditions within a garden, it is as well to understand just what situation and soil is required for successful fruit growing. For all kinds of fruit good drainage is essential, as waterlogging, even for short periods, at any time of the year can cause root death. On light to medium soils drainage is not usually a problem but on heavy clay soils it is likely to occur if some action is not taken. This may be difficult unless there is some lower ground close at hand to take the drainage water. For tree fruits the drainage needs to be effective at a depth of at least 1.2m (4ft), for the more vigorous rootstocks even deeper as the roots progress over the years far down into the sub-soil.

Established fruit trees may be extracting nutrients and moisture from as deep as 3m (10ft) and root die back at that depth can affect the long-term health of a tree. Cold air flows downhill and it is this downward flow that fills the valley with frosty air in April and May which is the critical blossoming time for most fruits. The removal of a short length of hedge or fencing in a small garden has been known to allow the cold air to flow away and so to reduce the risk of spring frost damage. Strawberries which grow close to the ground are very susceptible, their blossoms may be left with 'black eyes' whilst apple or pear blossom not more than 1m (3ft) higher up is undamaged.

Taking note of the need for good drainage for both water and air, it is evident that the fruit should ideally be grown on the highest part of the garden. Preparation of the ground before planting will, to a large extent, determine the degree of success ultimately achieved.

Drainage

If the land is likely to suffer from bad drainage the problem could possibly be reduced by putting in a series of land drains to channel the stagnant water away to lower ground. The trenches for the land drains should be about 1m (3ft) deep with a gradual fall to the lowest available ground. Clay land pipes, 5cm (2in) in diameter, laid end to end would be ideal, especially if they were given a covering of washed gravel before the trenches were filled in. Alternatively broken brick ends or rubble laid about 30cm (1ft) deep covered with washed gravel would allow the unwanted water to flow downhill. Directing the drainage water into a rubble-filled soakaway could be effective if the soil had some natural drainage ability but in solid clay it would become a reservoir of stagnant water. Whilst tree fruits would struggle if planted on raised mounds in a difficult drainage situation, strawberries and cane fruits with their shallower root systems could well succeed if the mounds were always above the possible stagnant water level.

Soil Preparation

On a normal site where the drainage is good, the ground should be prepared well ahead of the planting season, which extends from

November to March for plants lifted direct from the nursery with bare roots. The more expensive container-grown ones can, if well cared for at the nursery or garden centre, be planted at any time during the year but in general this is a less satisfactory approach to planting a complete fruit garden.

Whilst it is possible to deal with perennial weeds after planting fruit trees, when planting strawberries, cane or bush fruits the ground should be absolutely clear of perennial weeds such as couch grass, nettles, thistles and docks, before contemplating the planting. On dirty land a cleaning crop, such as potatoes, grown during the season before planting soft fruit or carrying out a fallow with several cultivations during the summer is best. Both approaches should be done in such a way that the weeds are never allowed to make above-ground growth. If weeds are denied the

opportuntiy to produce foliage they eventually die of exhaustion. An alternative approach would be to destroy the perennial weeds with a suitable weed killer whilst the ground is vacant and free of any crops, well before any planting is due to take place.

It is best to have the land ready a month ahead of planting time. This allows the soil to settle after it has been dug over. Then, with the land clean and dug to a depth of a full-size spade, all is ready for planting.

Planting

It is not advisable to apply a general fertiliser to the soil as newly-planted trees need time to develop an effective root system before being capable of absorbing nutrients in excess of those already present in the soil. However a sprinkling of bonemeal, a slow acting fertiliser, does help new root growth. Lime

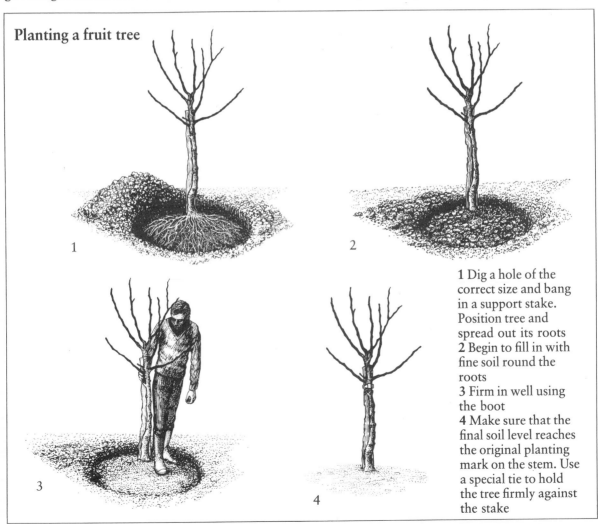

Planting a fruit tree

1 Dig a hole of the correct size and bang in a support stake. Position tree and spread out its roots
2 Begin to fill in with fine soil round the roots
3 Firm in well using the boot
4 Make sure that the final soil level reaches the original planting mark on the stem. Use a special tie to hold the tree firmly against the stake

should only be added to the soil when planting stoned-fruit trees (plums, cherries and peaches), but then only if the soil is acid. Whilst tree fruits are better without a lot of rich compost in the ground to start with, it is an advantage to incorporate some really well-rotted compost in ground intended for soft fruits. They will all thrive and above all it holds the moisture when the weather turns dry.

Good planting demands care. For fruit trees the hole should be large enough to accommodate the roots without cramping; the roots should be well distributed. The trees should be planted at the same depth as they were in the nursery, a soil mark on the stem will show this depth clearly. When filling in start with the finer soil, the idea being to work soil well in between the roots. A slight up-and-down movement of the tree stem will enable the soil to sift down between the roots. With the roots covered fill in the rest, firming down with the boot as you go, until it is level around the tree. It is a mistake to leave a sunken area around the tree to collect water.

Strawberries need to be planted with their crowns free of soil covering but not raised above ground level. The soil around them should be well firmed with the fingers. These same basic principles apply for planting cane and bush fruits. An important point to remember is that raspberries, cane fruits generally and black currants should be pruned back hard in March of the year following planting. This means no fruit in the first season but ensures that healthy and strong fruiting wood will be produced in subsequent years.

Planning the fruit plot
The fruit garden should be carefully planned so that the range of fruit grown is as wide as possible and the harvesting season extends from June to November. To achieve this the plot need be no larger than 6m by 3m (20ft by 10ft). In this small area there could be room to accommodate five cordon apples, one cordon pear, three cordon gooseberries, three cordon red currants, two black currant bushes, 10 summer-fruiting raspberries, 10 autumn-fruiting raspberries, 32 summer-fruiting strawberries, 12 autumn-fruiting strawberries plus two melons each year under cloches.

This is an example of intensive fruit growing in a limited area, but it is practical.

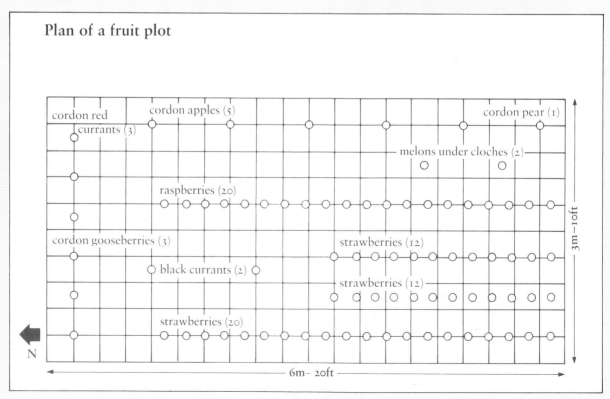

Plan of a fruit plot

cordon red currants (3)

cordon apples (5)

cordon pear (1)

melons under cloches (2)

raspberries (20)

cordon gooseberries (3)

strawberries (12)

black currants (2)

strawberries (12)

strawberries (20)

N

6m – 20ft

3m – 10ft

The bird problem

Above: The bullfinch is a great menace to the fruit grower

Left: a fruit cage is the only real answer to the bird problem

We have a working plot just like this at Clack's Farm. We pick our first crop of strawberries in June and go on producing fruit until the autumn, when we are still enjoying strawberries and raspberries. The apple harvest starts in August with Discovery and we still have Golden Delicious and Cox's Orange Pippin at Christmas.

To keep established fruit in good health and cropping regularly, supplementary feeding is essential. A number of suitable balanced fertilisers supplying the essential nutrients nitrogen, phosphates and potash are available. The time to apply them is important, otherwise they may not be present when they are needed most. The first application is made at the end of February. It is washed down to the roots and conditioned by the soil bacteria to coincide with the upward movement of the sap. At that time it really does benefit the swelling buds and the size of flower trusses; applied later it might be too late to be effective at this critical stage of growth.

The bird problem

At both ends of the season birds can be a problem. In the new year the bullfinches are, or can be, very destructive. They begin their attacks as soon as the bud scales indicate that growth is about to commence. First they start on the plums, after that they switch to pears and finally to apples before going on their way to feed on their normal diet of weed seeds. No fruit trees are absolutely safe when bullfinches abound in the district.

The blackbird and thrush problem begins at fruit ripening time. They seldom wait till the fruit is fully ripe before starting their raids. Having tried many methods of beating these raiders I have come to the conclusion that the only complete answer is overall netting.

TREE FRUITS

When a fruit tree is grown from a pip or a stone the root system and above-ground growth is usually extremely vigorous. This vigour results in a lot of wood growth and, more often than not, little or no fruit is produced. In the first instance new varieties are always raised from pips or stones, but for testing and cropping purposes budding or grafting on to a known rootstock is undertaken.

Rootstocks

Fruit trees produced for sale are always budded or grafted onto a rootstock. However rootstocks vary greatly in vigour so it is important to insist that the variety of your choice has been worked (grown) on a rootstock most suited to your needs and situation.

Thanks to the research and development programme at the East Malling Research station and the John Innes Horticultural Institute, a large number of rootstocks have been tested and classified. Data and knowledge concerning growth behaviour and cropping potential is now available and recent work on virus-free rootstocks opens up new horizons as regards to tree health and long-term profitable cropping.

A complete list of rootstocks would be lengthy and probably confusing, so for the garden fruit grower the short list which follows is of more practical help. For growing cordon apples on a really good soil my choice would be Malling 9 rootstock or Malling 26 rootstock. The latter is slightly more vigorous and therefore has a slightly less dwarfing effect on the tree. MM 106 rootstock is classed as semi-dwarfing and suitable for bush or espalier-grown trees. MM 111 is much more vigorous and recommended for larger trees grown as half-standards.

The choice of rootstocks suitable for pears is more limited. Quince C rootstock, which is now available guaranteed virus free, is less vigorous than Quince A and somewhat more willing to crop in the first few years.

Both apples and pears grown on dwarfing rootstocks must be kept staked and tied throughout their lives as their root systems are fibrous and do not provide sufficient anchorage to withstand the strains caused by either gales or heavy crops of fruit.

The new rootstocks Colt, for cherries, and Pixy, for plums, provide hope that in the future we may be able to grow these two stone fruits in limited areas without having to resort to drastic pruning at frequent intervals.

Training methods

Where space is limited apples and pears are best grown as single-stem cordons. For this the trees are planted at a sloping angle of 45° in rows 1m (3ft) apart. The idea of sloping the stem is to reduce the flow of sap. This encourages the development of more fruit buds and less wood growth, at the same time providing the opportunity to lengthen the fruit-bearing stem within a given height. To get the maximum benefit from the sun on cordon-grown fruit, the rows should run north to south with the trees sloped to the north. I prefer to plant maiden trees (one year old), older trees are more expensive and give little or no advantage as regards first cropping prospects.

Small free-standing bush trees on clean 1m (3ft) stems are very suitable for growing in gardens where space is limited. In this case it can be an advantage to purchase two-year-old trees which have been pruned to shape in the nursery. The same advice applies to the purchase of espaliers. This is a system of growing trees with their lateral branches trained horizontally along wires. Espalier growing can be recommended for gardens where a wall or fence is available, preferably one facing south or west.

Apples

Our climate is one of the best in the world for growing quality apples; the flesh quality and flavour of British-grown apples are superb. It is a crop that can be grown on most soils below an altitude of 180m (600ft); higher altitudes begin to present problems. Nevertheless, by planting varieties known to succeed in a certain district, the disadvantages can often be overcome.

The soil
Good soil drainage is essential as even short periods of waterlogging can cause die back of the roots. On heavy clay soils where drainage may be poor, canker (a fungus disease which eats into the branches) can be a possible problem although a degree of resistance to this is related to variety. Free drainage to a depth of 1.2m (4ft) is always necessary, but for trees on vigorous rootstocks this needs to be much deeper.

Fertility levels in soils vary greatly, but if the drainage is adequate it is not usually difficult to provide the nutrients in a balanced form to ensure good health and satisfactory cropping. Apples do well on soils with pH levels slightly below 7 (slightly acid); they are never really happy on chalky soils. Some very suitable top soils are known to overlie calcareous sub-soils in some places and in these situations the effect of the alkaline sub-soil may not be apparent during the first few years growth. On chalky soils the foliage is liable to become chlorotic (it becomes yellow due to the lack of production of chlorophyll, the green pigment). This condition can often be corrected by seasonal spraying with chelated iron or manganese.

The site
The secret of successful apple growing is to appreciate the restrictions likely to be imposed by the site and prepare the ground accordingly. Make sure that the trees you plant are on the appropriate rootstocks (see page 78) and that the varieties are suitable for the district. If possible avoid planting apples in a vegetable growing area, as the nitrogen level present in the soil for vegetable growing would be far too high for quality dessert apples.

Another factor which affects the quality of dessert apples is rainfall; 63cm (25in) annual rainfall is regarded as just about right. In districts where 100cm (40in) and above are experienced it is wise to concentrate on culinary varieties. Most gardens do afford some protection against the full force of the wind but plantings on exposed sites could benefit from a shelter belt on the south-west side. However, it is a mistake to plant new fruit trees too close to established trees or buildings.

In coastal districts protection against wind can be more difficult as salt-laden air becomes an additional problem. In a garden where there is a choice of site, always plant on the higher ground. This will reduce the risk of spring frost damage as cold air flows, like water, downhill. It is a wise precaution to cut an opening in a hedge or fence so that the colder air can flow away from the fruit area.

Planting distances
In a garden there is often a tendency to plant fruit trees too close together. This usually results in the trees having to be drastically cut back just as they are coming into full bearing. It is much better to allow adequate space for the ultimate size of each tree. To avoid wasting the space you can intercrop with soft fruit during the first years. Bush trees on either Malling 9 or 26 rootstocks can be planted 3m (10ft) apart. Those on MM 106 rootstock, which is more vigorous, should be at least 3.7m (12ft) apart, but thinking of the future, 5.5m (18ft) would be much better.

Dwarf pyramid trees demand more expertise in pruning and can be planted as close as 1.2m (4ft) apart, again they should be on either Malling 9 or Malling 26 rootstock. For half-standard trees on more vigorous rootstocks, such as MM 111, 7.2m (24ft) or even more apart would be required. Trained espalier trees on MM 106 rootstock need at least 2.5m (8ft) clear on either side of the main stem for development of fruiting laterals. Cordon-trained trees can be spaced at 1m (3ft) apart.

Feeding
After the roots have established themselves,

apple trees need a regular annual balanced-fertiliser application. I apply Growmore at the rate of 60 to 90g per sq m (2 to 3oz per sq yd). The best time to give this is late February when the sap is beginning to rise; later applications are often less valuable unless watered in. Potash is very important especially for Cox's Orange Pippin.

Pruning

The pruning of a newly-planted maiden tree determines its future shape. For a bush tree to grow on a 60cm (2ft) stem the main leader should be cut back to 1m (3ft). If older trees are purchased these would only need their branches shortening by about half to encourage an extension of the branch framework.

Hard pruning in established trees results in more wood growth and can be just as wrong as haphazard snipping around with a pair of secateurs. Right from the start the pruning should be designed to allow access of light and air; quality fruit needs plenty of sunlight. In older trees this may mean cutting out crossing branches with a saw, such wounds that result should be painted with a wound paint. Winter is the best time to prune apples. However do remember that some apples are tip bearers, the fruit buds are at the very ends of the branches. Fruit buds are quite a lot fatter than leaf buds and you must be careful not to prune them all out or the following crop will be lost.

Pest and Diseases

A complete list will be found in the charts on pages 87 and 120. By using insecticides and fungicides that are safe to the user, the consumer and domestic pets and wild life, it is possible to control the most important pests and diseases by spraying. However, do follow the manufacturer's instructions to the letter. There is no reason why apples should be maggoty or scabby, it is just a question of applying the right product at the right time. A sprayer capable of covering the whole of the tree with spray is essential.

Harvesting

Apples for storing must mature on the tree and should not be picked until the stalk parts easily from the branch. Any bruised and imperfect fruit should be set aside for immediate use and not be stored. Store apples in a cool airy place in a single layer, wrapping individual fruit in paper to prevent spreading of disease. Special oiled papers can be purchased for this purpose.

Varieties

Below is a limited list selected for garden cultivation.

Dessert

Blenheim Orange: an old favourite, large

1 Rev. W. Wilks
(culinary)
2 Discovery (dessert)
3 James Grieve
(dessert)
4 Lane's Prince Albert
(culinary)

flattish apple, skin yellow with a dull red flush, flesh yellow, crisp with a nutty flavour. Self-sterile so needs two pollinators to blossom at the same time. Season: November/January. Mid-season flowering.

Charles Ross: a reliable cropper, large fruit, skin pale yellow with red stripes and flush. Flesh is sweet and tender, tends to go woolly in store. Does better than most on a chalky soil. Season: October/December. Mid-season flowering.

Cox's Orange Pippin: the number one dessert apple, superb flavour, more difficult to grow than most. For good growth and fruit size, potash is essential. Particularly susceptible to scab and mildew. Season: November/January. Mid-season flowering.

Discovery: medium-sized flattish fruit, skin yellow to red. Flesh is firm with a superb flavour. Needs netting against birds. Tip bearing. Season: mid-August/September. Mid-season flowering.

Egremont Russet: a true russet, flesh yellow and juicy, excellent flavour. Susceptible to boron deficiency which causes cracking. Season: October/December. Early flowering.

Epicure: on it's day a truly delicious apple, medium-sized flattish fruit, skin greenish-yellow flushed red. Often needs thinning. Aromatic flavour. Season: September. Mid-season flowering.

Fortune: a good cropper in some districts, medium-sized fruit, skin yellow with red streaks, unique aromatic flavour. Season: September/October. Mid-season flowering.

Idared: a free cropper, medium-sized fruit, good reddish colour. Excellent keeper, when fully ripe a good flavour and sweet. Suitable for cooking. Susceptible to mildew. Season: November/April. Early flowering.

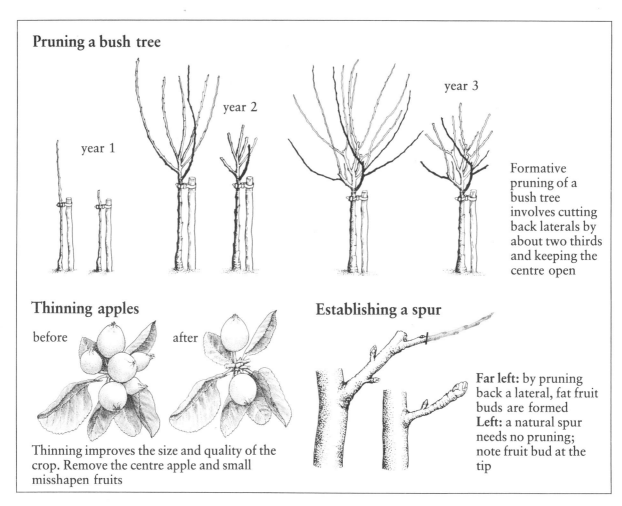

Pruning a bush tree

year 1

year 2

year 3

Formative pruning of a bush tree involves cutting back laterals by about two thirds and keeping the centre open

Thinning apples

before

after

Thinning improves the size and quality of the crop. Remove the centre apple and small misshapen fruits

Establishing a spur

Far left: by pruning back a lateral, fat fruit buds are formed
Left: a natural spur needs no pruning; note fruit bud at the tip

James Grieve: the most popular garden apple, free cropper, medium-sized fruit. When ripe on the tree it is yellowish red, delicious flavour but deteriorates quickly after picking. Bruises easily. Season: September/early October. Mid-season flowering.

Lord Lambourne: a regular cropper, slightly flattish fruit of medium size, dull yellow skin with crimson flush and streaks. Flesh firm, excellent flavour. Season: October/November. Early flowering.

Red Ellison: tends to be a biennial cropper, good sized fruit, skin bright red, flesh inclined to be soft. Aromatic flavour with a hint of aniseed in it. Season: September/ October. Late flowering.

Sunset: this is the alternative to Cox's Orange Pippin in less favourable districts. The flattish fruit is inclined to be small unless thinned. Skin golden yellow with reddish flush and russet specks. Flesh very firm, excellent flavour. Keeps well. Season:

November/December. Mid-season flowering.

Superb (Laxton's Superb): a biennial cropper with tremendous potential, its vigorous whippy growth is against it in small gardens. Good-sized fruit, skin greenish-yellow with red flush. Flesh firm with fair flavour. Season: November/February. Mid-season flowering.

Worcester Pearmain: still popular as a garden apple, should be picked and eaten ripe from the tree when it is full of juice, sweetness and flavour. Goes woolly in store and loses its flavour. A tip bearer. Season: August/September. Late flowering.

Culinary

Arthur Turner: sometimes grown solely for its ornamental blossom, a regular cropper with round to conical shaped fruit, skin greenish-yellow with brownish-red flush. Flesh white, fair flavour and cooking qualities. Season: August/October. Mid-season flowering.

Bramley's Seedling: the finest late keeper, very

vigorous unless planted on a dwarfing rootstock, susceptible to spring frosts and scab. Needs two pollinators nearby which blossom at the same time. Very large flat fruit, skin green, flesh firm, excellent cooking qualities. Heavy cropper when conditions suit it. Season: November/March. Mid-season flowering.

Early Victoria: usually planted on account of its earliness, tends to be a biennial cropper and to need thinning in its 'on' (cropping) year. Medium-sized conical fruit, skin yellowish green, flesh greenish white. Cooks down to a delicious froth. July thinnings cook well. Season: July/August. Mid-season flowering.

Grenadier: a larger apple than Early Victoria and about a month later. Regular cropper, good-sized round- to conical-shaped fruit, skin greenish-yellow, flesh white, goes down to a froth when cooked, good flavour. Season: August/September. Mid-season flowering.

Howgate Wonder: a vigorous grower, a regular and heavy cropper. Fruit very large;

skin yellowish-green with a slight red flush and streaks. Frothy when cooked but lacks flavour. Season: November/February. Mid-season flowering.

Lane's Prince Albert: a regular cropper which lost popularity on account of lime sulphur sensitivity, should now be more widely grown. Large roundish fruits, skin greenish-yellow with red streaks, flesh greenish-white, cooks superbly and is an excellent alternative to Bramley's Seedling for a small garden. Season: November/March. Late flowering.

Lord Derby: always a regular cropper, large oblong conical fruit, greenish-yellow skin, firm white flesh, cooks well, excellent flavour. Will set its fruit without pips, short keeping life. Season: October/November. Late flowering.

Rev. W. Wilks: a biennial cropper which may need thinning in its 'on year', very large apple of great quality, creamy white skin with slight flushing, flesh white and soft. Superb baking and cooking qualities with unequalled flavour. An acceptable dessert apple when

Pruning cordon apples

Formative pruning of a cordon after planting a one-year-old tree. Plant cordons 1m (3ft) apart with the scion on top. This ensures there is less pressure on the scion, making a break at the join unlikely

year 1   year 2   years 3

before   after

Summer pruning of cordons

This operation should not be carried out until the first or second week of August when the wood is hard. If you prune too early fruit buds will break into leafy growth resulting in a greatly reduced crop the following year. Pruning involves cutting back the laterals in order to produce fruiting spurs

fully ripe. Season: September/October. Early
flowering.

The choice of varieties will, or should be,
determined by the district in which you live
and the situation within the garden. In the
southern half of the country most varieties
can be grown successfully but in the less
favoured districts it is important to be
selective when preparing a planting list.
Accepting the usual dividing line of climatic
change, the River Trent across to the Severn
estuary; north of this line the average
temperatures are lower and hours of sunshine
less, so try the following:
Dessert: Charles Ross, Discovery, Egremont
Russet, Epicure, Fortune, James Grieve, Lord
Lambourne, Red Ellison and Worcester
Pearmain.
Culinary: Arthur Turner, Grenadier, Lord
Derby and Rev. W. Wilks.
For planting in gardens (anywhere in the
country) particularly susceptible to spring
frosts, it is worthwhile to consider varieties
with blossom that is less affected. These are:
Dessert: Discovery, Epicure, James Grieve,

Red Ellison, Worcester Pearmain.
Culinary: Lord Derby.
For the gardener who wants to grow apples
with the minimum care try:
Dessert: Charles Ross, Discovery, Egremont
Russet, Epicure, Fortune, Red Ellison, Sunset.
Culinary: Grenadier and Rev. W. Wilks.

Crab Apples

For the fruit grower it can be an advantage to
have a crab apple tree close at hand as some
varieties are particularly good pollinators.
The most popular variety is John Downie but
for pollination there is none better than the
very small-fruited Golden Hornet.
One of the best varieties for making jelly is
Yellow Siberian. The large-fruited variety
Wisley Crab, with its wine-red flowers and
reddish coloured leaves, has large purple-
skinned, pink-fleshed fruits which make a
good quality rosé wine if gathered and used
quickly after ripening. They are all, in any
case, attractive specimen trees for the garden
in their own right.

1 Louise Bonne de Jersey
2 Clapp's Favourite
3 Williams' Bon Crétien
4 Beurré Hardy
5 Conference

Pears

Pear and apple trees have much in common, including their cultivation, methods of pruning and many of the pests and diseases that attack them; however there are a few additional points to bear in mind. Pear trees are not difficult to grow but the question of fruiting them successfully must be considered as so much depends on climatic conditions.

In a well-drained soil, especially if it is one capable of holding moisture during the summer, the trees will be happy enough. For fruiting, especially dessert varieties, warmth and plenty of sunshine during the growing season is needed; for this reason the south-east of Great Britain is the best pear growing area. Above the oft quoted Trent/Severn line it is wise to plant trained trees against south or west facing walls or fences rather than out in the open.

Another point to remember is that pears blossom earlier than apples and so are even more susceptible to spring frost damage.

Planting in frost pockets can have very disappointing results. Pear foliage is tender and easily damaged by gale force winds so trees in exposed positions benefit from protection.

Rootstocks

Dwarfing rootstocks for pears are limited but there is no need to plant standard trees which take years to come into fruiting and need ladders to pick the crop. Bush trees worked on Quince C rootstock are the least vigorous and can be planted 4m (13ft) apart but the trees will need to be staked and tied for life. Quince A rootstock is more vigorous and probably more freely available; the planting distance for bush trees on this stock should be 5.5m (18ft). Either rootstock is suitable for cordons or trained trees; however on less fertile soils Quince A would be the better choice. Whilst established apples are quite happy growing in grass, pears do best in clean cultivated land. Therefore keep a large circle of cultivated soil round the trees.

Pruning

Generally speaking pears dislike pruning, whilst it is necessary the less severely it is done the better for continuity of cropping. Pruning of pears is carried out in the same way as for apples (see pages 82 and 83).

Feeding

A balanced fertiliser application late February will help to maintain tree health and cropping. Apply Growmore at the rate of 70 to 100 per sq m (2 to 3oz per sq yd).

Pests and Diseases

See spraying charts opposite and on page 120.

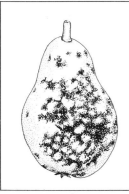

Pear scab

This disease manifests itself as blackish marks on the fruit. In severe cases cracking can occur. The foliage becomes blotchy and shoots develop scabby patches

Harvesting

All pears should be picked before they are fully ripe. The correct time is when the fruit stalk parts easily from the branch, a slight lifting of the pear will indicate the right moment. Remember though, the whole crop will not necessarily be ready at the same time. Handle the fruit with great care and store in a cool airy place in a single layer. Check daily for peak ripeness to enjoy them at their best, as they become over-ripe very quickly.

Varieties

In choosing varieties pollination should be considered, with few exceptions such as Conference and Fertility most need one and sometimes two other varieties nearby which blossom at the same time.

Beurré Hardy: a vigorous heavy cropper, fruit large, skin greenish-yellow with russeted patches and red flush. Excellent flavour, plenty of juice when fully ripe. Season: October. Mid-season flowering.

Catillac: a vigorous regular cropper, large roundish fruit, the best cooking pear. Keeps well. Season: December/April. Late flowering.

Conference: this is the number one garden pear, self-fertile, reliable cropper, fruit is medium sized with long neck. The skin is dark green and russeted. Very juicy and sweet when ripe. Season: October/November. Mid-season flowering.

Fertility: a regular cropper, skin dull yellow russeted, fruit lacks flavour. Season: October. Mid-season flowering.

Louise Bonne de Jersey: a good garden variety, regular cropper, fruit medium sized, skin yellow/green flushed with red, excellent flavour. Season: October. Early flowering.

Onward: a new variety which has Comice as one of its parents. Its fruit is similar in shape, colour and flavour and it could become popular. Season: Early September. Late flowering.

Williams' Bon Chrétien: a vigorous tree, free cropper, medium-sized fruit, skin golden/yellow with russet and slight red streaks when ripe. Excellent flavour. Season: September. Mid-season flowering.

Winter Nellis: a good cropper, fruit small, skin yellow with dark spots when ripe, good flavour, excellent keeper. Season: November/January. Late flowering.

Spray Chart for Apples and Pears

Appearance of buds	Stage	Pest or Disease	Chemical
	dormant	eggs of overwintering insects	tar oil winter wash
	bud burst	red spider mite aphids scab	dinocap malathion or a systemic insecticide captan
	green bud	red spider mite suckers and aphids scab	dinocap malathion or a systemic insecticide captan
	pink bud (apples) white bud (pears)	red spider mite suckers and aphids scab	dinocap malathion or a systemic insecticide captan
	open flower	never spray at this stage to avoid killing bees and other pollinating insects	
	petal fall	codling moth red spider mite aphids scab	fenitrothion dinocap malathion or a systemic insecticide captan
	fruitlet	codling moth red spider mite aphids scab	fenitrothion dinocap malathion or a systemic insecticide captan

Cherries

Before embarking upon a scheme for planting cherries it is wise to consider the blackbird problem and how to overcome it. So without complete protection against blackbirds it is a total waste of time to plant either sweet or sour cherries.

This means that free-standing trees are not a practical proposition in a small garden, as they are vigorous growers and become large trees and almost impossible to protect by the time they have developed their full cropping capacity. However, trained trees against a wall or fence which can be entirely netted are suitable for the smaller garden, especially if they are grown on the recently introduced Colt rootstock. This new dwarfing rootstock

Pruning a fan-trained cherry

before

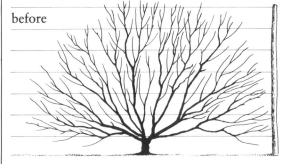

The aim of pruning and training is to achieve an even distribution of branches

after

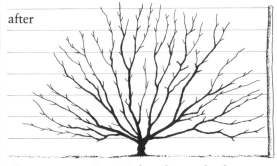

Carry out pruning in July to lessen the danger of infection by silver leaf disease. Any weak or damaged growth should be cut out, together with shoots growing directly backwards or forwards if these have not been rubbed out earlier. Congested growth should be thinned out and those laterals to be retained shortened to five leaves and tied in

has vigour roughly comparable to that of the well known and popular MM 106 apple rootstock. Cherries on Colt rootstock are a good choice for trained trees where excess wood growth would create problems.

Growing conditions

Whilst cherries are not difficult to grow they are more exacting than most other fruits when it comes to successful cropping. The drainage needs to be efficient, a deep loam overlying chalk is ideal, such as that found in parts of Kent. Cherries blossom early, this means that low-lying districts noted either for spring frosts or cold winds are not very suitable. Here again, planting in a protected position can overcome these disadvantages.

Warm weather conditions during the growing season produces the finest quality cherries and the heaviest crops. This means that the south-east of England is undoubtedly the most favourable district, but there again trained trees with protection can be grown well elsewhere in the southern half of the country. For sweet cherries a south- or west-facing fence or wall is best but Morello cherries crop well in sunless positions even against a north wall. All will need watering from time to time during the growing season.

Planting

As with all other fruit trees November is the best month to plant, but it can be done at any time during the dormant season provided the soil is in good condition.

Only container-grown trees can be planted during the growing season. Unless the soil is chalky it is an advantage to apply some garden lime to the planting area before starting, 230g per sq m (8ozs per sq yd) would be suitable application rate. On acid soils additional applications of garden lime will be needed every other year to keep the trees healthy and to ensure successful stoning.

Whilst I prefer to plant maiden (one-year-old) trees and train them myself, it is simpler to purchase two-year-old or even older trees which have been fan trained in the nursery.

Pruning and training

An open fan should be formed of main branches evenly spread out against supporting wires fixed onto the wall. These

Opposite: A fan-trained Morello cherry
Inset: Morello cherries

leaders should have their tips taken out when they have reached the required height or the top of the wall. Training of sub-laterals is carried out by tying in the retained growths which should be shortened to five leaves in July and to three or four buds after fruiting has taken place. Any buds that are growing either directly outwards or in towards the wall should be rubbed out early in the season. Any weak or damaged growth should be removed. This training operation is best carried out during the growing season when the risk of silver leaf disease and bacterial canker is at its lowest level.

If in old trees it is necessary to cut out large branches, the saw cuts should be painted immediately with a bitumen or tree wound paint. Remember when pruning that sour cherries fruit on one-year-old wood while sweet cherries produce on older growth.

Feeding
As all cherries tend to make a lot of wood growth, nitrogenous fertilisers should be used sparingly, whereas potash (sulphate of potash) and phosphates (super phosphate) can be applied with advantage. The best time to apply fertiliser is in February.

Varieties
Sweet cherries
*Merton Glory: bright red, creamy white flesh, good flavour.
*Early Rivers: large fruit, deep crimson/black, good flavour when fully ripe.
*Noir de Guben: large fruit, blackish/red, moderate flavour.
*universal pollinators: plant at least two varieties for cross pollination.
Sour cherry
Morello: deep-red fruit; self fertile.

Plums and Damsons

Plums and damsons are our most hardy stone fruits, both do best on medium to heavy soils provided the drainage is satisfactory. On light soils which are subject to drying out established trees will need artificial watering to keep the fruit swelling and prevent it from shrivelling up. Another possible problem on light soils could be lack of calcium—an essential element for the health of the tree and for the development of stones. If in doubt apply garden lime at the rate of 120 to 230g per sq m (4 to 8ozs per sq yd) before planting and repeat every two or three years.

I prefer to grow plums and damsons in clean cultivated land throughout their lives as both seem to object to having their roots covered either by grass or weeds. Both plums and damsons blossom early in March or April depending on the season. The blossom is susceptible to spring frost damage which is usually more severe in low lying areas as the cold air flows downwards. Therefore always try to plant plum trees on the highest ground on your plot to ensure that the frost can escape through a gap in a hedge or fence.

Rootstocks
Several rootstocks are used for plums and damsons including St Julian A which is semi-dwarfing and suitable for all types of trees, free-standing or fan-trained. St Julian Seedling is more vigorous than St Julian A. Myrobalan, which is still more vigorous, is commonly used for damsons.

Pruning
In the first few years free-standing plum trees tend to make a lot of strong wood growth, this should be left without pruning and the trees allowed to settle down to fruiting. By spacing plum trees 5.5m (18ft) apart and damsons 4.2m (14ft) apart you avoid the need for cutting the trees back.

In general pruning should be restricted to removal of crossing branches and dead wood. Any large wounds created by saw cuts should be treated immediately with a wound or bitumen paint to prevent 'silver leaf' infection. The safest time to do such jobs is at the beginning of the growing season when the sap is beginning to flow.

Fan-trained plums can be grown against a wall or fence, preferably south- or west-facing. Pruning and training is carried out as for cherries, although training needs to be very carefully and regularly done by rubbing

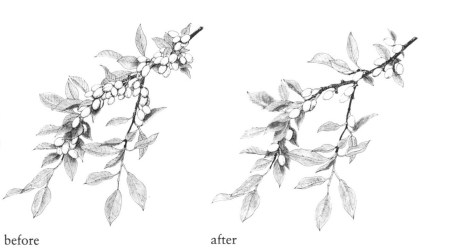

Thinning plums

It is wise to thin a heavy crop of plums in order to obtain fruits of better size and flavour and to prevent broken branches. Start to thin at the beginning of June and complete the job at the end of the month after the natural drop has taken place

before

after

out unwanted soft green shoots rather than resorting to the secateurs. The great advantage of this trained form of tree is that it can be completely netted against attack from marauding birds and protected from frost.

Pests and diseases

The most troublesome problem can be the bullfinches, they systematically strip the swelling fruit buds early in the New Year soon after the buds being to swell. In districts where bullfinches operate the growing of fan-trained trees which can be completely netted is the answer. Trees planted in November should whilst still dormant be sprayed with a tar oil winter wash. This treatment destroys aphid and caterpillar eggs on the wood; by repeating the application each winter the tree will be kept relatively clean.

Silver Leaf is a disease caused by a fungus, it is very infectious and covered by a 'Silver Leaf Order 1923' which requires the removal and burning of infected dead wood before the 15th July. The disease causes dieback and the leaves appear silvery. Infected wood shows a purplish stain in the inner wood. Infected wood should not be left lying about as the fungus fructifications can spread the disease over a wide area.

Varieties

Some varieties of plums and damsons are self-fertile, but many need to be cross-pollinated.

If this is the case plant varieties that flower at the same time to ensure fruit production.

Plums

Green Gage: olive green with slight red flush and spots, delicious flavour, unreliable cropper. Season: August/September. Late flowering.
Jefferson: large, golden flushed and red spotted some russet patches. Excellent flavour, reliable cropper. Season: September. Early flowering.
Kirke's: fairly large, purple with blue bloom, superb flavour, ideal for a warm wall. Season: September. Mid-season flowering.
Transparent Gage: medium golden-yellow slightly flushed violet, aromatic flavour, best on a warm wall. Season: September. Mid-season flowering.
Victoria: large bright red with spots when ripe, cooks well, moderate flavour. The variety for a one plum tree garden. Season: August/September. Mid-season flowering. Self-fertile.

Damsons

Shropshire Damson (Prune Damson): small true damson, moderate cropper, makes a small tree. Season: September/October. Late flowering. Self-fertile.
Merryweather Damson: large oval fruits, fair flavour. Season: September. Mid-season flowering. Self-fertile.

CANE FRUITS

There is no doubt about the popularity of raspberries which has increased with the universal introduction of deep freezers; no other fruit comes out in such good condition. However this is no reason for disregarding blackberries, loganberries and some of the hybrid berries, especially as all of them can be grown practically anywhere in the country.

Growing conditions

As regards growing conditions their needs are virtually the same, a medium well-drained loam would be ideal but other soils ranging from light to heavy can be developed to grow any of the cane fruits successfully. Good drainage is essential as waterlogging kills the roots, but on the other hand dry soil conditions check growth and fruit production. Whilst an open sunny position is best, all cane fruits will crop in partial shade but planting in full shade should be avoided.

Thorough preparation of the site before planting is extremely important and how well this job is done will to a large extent determine the degree of success over the next few years. The ground should be deeply dug early in the autumn and cleared of all perennial weed roots; couch grass especially can become a real problem if its living rhizomes are turned in. On a very weedy site it could be better to wait a year and grow a cleaning crop, such as potatoes, on the area before planting the cane fruits the following autumn.

Well-rotted compost or manure incorporated during the digging operation will not only improve the fertility but also the moisture-holding capacity of the soil during the growing season. Only in very exceptional situations where the soil is extremely acid or sour would I recommend the pre-planting use of garden lime. Cane fruits generally do best when the soil has a high organic content and is slightly acid, about pH 6 to 6.5.

Virus problems

All cane fruits are susceptible to virus diseases but none more so than raspberries. Once a plant is infected it loses vigour gradually until it becomes unfruitful. Virus diseases are spread mainly by sucking insects, such as aphids, which feed on an infected plant then move on to infect healthy plants. It is wise to start with healthy stock, plants carrying a Ministry of Agriculture certificate of Health. Then from the word go to make sure that sucking insects (greenfly, leafhoppers) are completely controlled; a monthly application of a systemic greenfly killer will do this.

Planting

November is about the best time for this but the normal planting season goes on until March. The earlier planting results in new root development well ahead of the growing season and avoids the stress of above and below ground growth starting simultaneously. Whenever the planting is done be sure that the soil is in a reasonable condition, certainly not too wet. If the plants arrive when conditions are unsuitable for planting, heel them in by digging a trench and

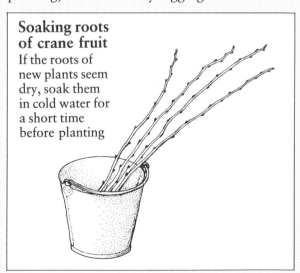

Soaking roots of crane fruit
If the roots of new plants seem dry, soak them in cold water for a short time before planting

Opposite: The blackberry Oregon Thornless

92

laying the plants in it, covering their roots with soil. If frost prevents heeling-in, keep the roots moist and store under cover until planting is possible.

A small handful of bonemeal worked into the planting holes will help root growth, but no other fertiliser is needed at this time. If the roots appear dry, a few minutes soak in a bucket of cold water prior to planting is advisable. The roots should be spread out in the planting holes, which are then filled in working fine soil well between the roots. Then use the gardener's boot to firm the soil down around the plant to complete the job. Ensure the soil surface is level and no hollow remains to collect water.

Care and cultivation

In the first growing season the aim should be to produce good strong canes for fruiting the following year. This is done by cutting the newly planted canes back to 15cm (6in) above ground in March. All cane fruits are surface rooting, so digging between rows or close to the plants should be avoided. Surface cultivation for weed control should be done carefully using a Dutch hoe.

Established canes appreciate a mulch with well-rotted compost or manure but it should be applied when the soil is moist. The best time for applying supplementary food is March. Use a balanced fertiliser such as Growmore at the rate of 100 to 120g per sq m (3 to 4oz per sq yd).

Blackberries

Accepting the fact that no cultivated blackberry has quite the flavour of its hedgerow relative, the cropping ability of the garden versions make up for the slight shortcomings of flavour.

Since the introduction of Himalayan Giant, with its enormous vigour and terrible thorns, much has happened in the plant breeding world. We now have a selection of thornless blackberries that crop consistently well and have acceptable flavour. All varieties need to be fully ripe when picked. They all freeze well.

Pruning and Training

In common with other cane fruits the land

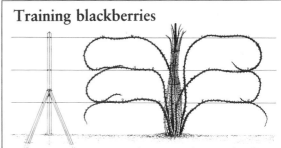

Training blackberries

Train canes along taut horizontal wires, leading new growth up a central stick. After fruiting cut down old canes

must be well drained but blackberries do crop well in partial shade. Some form of support is needed for training. I use posts and three strands of horizontal wires 60cm (2ft) apart. The modern thornless varieties can be planted 4m (13ft) apart whereas Himalayan Giant would need twice this space.

After planting during the dormant season, November for preference, a newly-planted cane is cut down in March to a good bud near to ground level. The young cane growth develops quickly and is tied in to the wires on both sides of the plant for fruiting the following season. In the case of established blackberries the new young canes should be kept off the ground out of harms' way. I tie them to 2.5m (8ft) bamboo canes. Immediately after cropping when the old canes are cut out, I select six of the best young canes as replacements, tying in three on each side of the plant, if they need more than the 2m (6ft) available I loop them back.

Pests

Raspberry beetle can be a problem but derris, as for raspberries, provides the answer.

Varieties

Bedford Giant: vigorous and prickly, berries sweet and juicy. Season: July to August.
Himalayan Giant: very vigorous and thorny, heavy cropper of fair flavour. Season: September.
Merton Thornless: moderate vigour, fair cropper, good flavoured sweet berries but needs to be well grown. Season: August to September.
Oregon Thornless: moderate vigour, fair cropper, distinctive parsley leaved foliage, good flavour. Season: August to September.

Raspberries

By planting both summer- and autumn-fruiting raspberries a long season of cropping can be ensured of these delicious fruits. Autumn-fruiting varieties do not crop so heavily as the summer fruiters, but in both cases the fruits should be picked fully ripe and dry, especially for freezing.

Summer fruiting

For these I erect a row of support posts with three horizontal strands of round wire, the top wire at 1.5m (5ft) with the lower wires spaced 45cm (18in) apart. The planting distances I use are 45cm (18in) between plants and 2m (6ft) between the rows. All newly-planted raspberries should be cut back to 15cm (6in) in March.

Summer-fruiting varieties will only produce new canes that year and no fruit. In subsequent seasons all the old canes are cut out immediately after fruiting to allow the young canes space to develop. After cutting out the old canes in summer-fruiting varieties, I select, if possible, five of the strongest young canes and loosely tie these to the three support wires, at the same time discarding the weaker surplus canes. At the end of the year I check the ties and cut back any very tall canes

Pruning raspberries

Summer-fruiting raspberries should be tied to taut wires. After fruiting, cut out old canes

to just above the height of the top wire.

Autumn fruiting

I have found temporary support stakes with a length of strong string run along both sides of the canes sufficient to support these late-fruiting raspberries. These are planted 45cm (18in) apart and a gap of 2m (6ft) left between rows — the same spacing as for the summer fruiters in fact. Similarly autumn-fruiting varieties should be cut back to 15cm (6in) in March but they will produce both new canes and fruit in the first season after planting. In the following years all the canes are cut down to ground level in February or March and a new flush of canes will follow to fruit in the autumn.

Pests

The chief pest apart from the birds is raspberry beetle, which is responsible for the maggots sometimes found in the berries. Derris insecticide applied at the white flower bud stage and repeated at petal fall will control it. To avoid harming bees, do not spray fully open blossom.

Complete overall netting against birds is usually necessary for summer-fruiting varieties but judging by our own experience the autumn-fruiting varieties are less attractive to the blackbirds.

Varieties
Summer fruiting

Glen Cova: a very vigorous tall grower, new canes tend to make picking difficult, on account of its susceptibility to virus disease it should be grown on its own. Good flavour.

Lloyd George: very susceptible to virus disease, essential to obtain certified plants, will also fruit on young canes in the autumn, good flavour.

Malling Admiral: late season, large berries but poor flavour.

Malling Delight: mid-season, good cropper with extra large berries. Superb exhibition variety. Poor flavour.

Malling Jewel: mid-season, good cropper, throws its fruit clear of the foliage. The number one variety for flavour.

Malling Promise: early, heavy cropper, rather soft berries of good flavour.

Norfolk Giant: late, tall strong canes, heavy

cropper, often a virus carrier but fairly resistant, fair flavour.

Autumn fruiting
Fall Gold: October, small golden-yellow berries but a light cropper, excellent flavour.
Heritage: September to October, very good cropper, firm berries, good flavour, erect canes.
September: September to October, high quality round berries, medium cropper, excellent flavour.
Zeva: October, good cropper, large soft berries of good flavour, strong canes.

Hybrid Berries

There are a number of these hybrid berries available. They are usually the result of raspberry-blackberry crosses. These are the most popular kinds.

Loganberries

The cultivation and treatment of the canes are the same as for blackberries. However loganberries seem to prefer organically-based fertilisers for the March application. I have used a fish, blood and bone product with success.

The original loganberry was slightly thorned and uncomfortable to handle, it came to this country from Oregon where it was said to have resulted from a cross between a blackberry and a raspberry. As it is a hybrid there are no varieties as such, but by selection a thornless version has emerged and is now the one generally planted. The thornless loganberry is vigorous, the berries are large, with just the same flavour and fruit quality as the original one.

Raspberry beetle does occasionally attack loganberries but, as for raspberries, the double application of derris at white bud and petal fall ensures clean fruit. To really enjoy loganberries they must be picked fully ripe, for either immediate use or freezing.

Right: Japanese wineberries
Opposite: Loganberries are vigorous plants and need to be trained to be kept under control. Leave an open centre for new growth to develop

96

Boysenberries

Another hybrid berry from America and reported to be a three-way cross involving loganberry, blackberry and raspberry. It was raised in California about 1930. Cultivation is generally the same as for a loganberry. The large berries are purplish-black when fully ripe, when the flavour is delicious. It fruits during July and August.

Youngberries

A hybrid of American origin, very similar to the Boysenberry but the berries are slightly more round. The flavour is excellent and it produces fruit during July and August.

Japanese Wineberry

This is also known as the Chinese blackberry. A very decorative plant native to Japan. It is not a hybrid but cultivated in the same way as loganberries. The golden-yellow berries are round and of medium size, turning to wine-red when fully ripe. It has a sweet and pleasant flavour and the fruit is ready for harvesting in July and August.

BUSH FRUITS

By their very nature currants, black, red or white, and gooseberries are well worth a place in a small garden as the space required to grow them will always be more than justified by the yearly crop yields. They are all relatively easy to grow but to get the best results their needs and habits should be understood.

Growing conditions

A well-drained soil is a basic general requirement. Black currants are more demanding as regards soil fertility but this is something that the gardener can deal with on practically any type of soil. The pre-planting treatment of the ground is important, especially as all the bush fruits suffer if the soil moisture level drops too low during the growing season.

On all types of soil, heavy or light, the incorporation of well-rotted compost or manure has great advantages, especially if it is dug in several weeks in advance of planting. The deeper the land is dug the better, but a single spade depth is sufficient, provided the blade of the spade is full length and not just a shadow of its former self. The best month for planting is November.

All bush fruits blossom early, so plantings in particularly low-lying areas are more prone to spring frost damage, however a short period of giving protection to a few small bushes is not too arduous a task. Protecting cordon-trained bush fruits against spring frosts and bird damage is, of course, easier but this cannot apply to black currants.

Growing as cordons

Whereas red and white currants and gooseberries fruit on old wood, black currants fruit on the previous season's growth which would be removed each year if we attempted to grow them in the usual cordon fashion. So although all can be grown as bushes, only red and white currants and gooseberries can be grown as cordons.

Cordons take up little space when planted 38cm (15in) apart in the row and given the support of horizontal wiring. I prefer to start with one-year-old plants as older plants have usually been allowed to develop along bush lines in the nursery. They should be planted sloping to the north at an angle of 45°. This ensures the cordons get the maximum amount of sunshine and the sap flow is slightly slower, resulting in better fruiting.

One-year-old plants have a single stem with only a few laterals so it is easy to loosely tie in the stem to the wires. To facilitate this I first tie in a bamboo cane at the correct angle to the wires and then tie the cordon to the cane. The laterals are then shortened to about 5cm (2in). In subsequent years the laterals are allowed to develop during the growing season but are cut back again in the autumn. If this is carried out too early secondary shoots will result which will be still immature at the onset of winter.

Black Currants

These are the gross feeders. They need good growing conditions all the time. A medium to light loam liberally supplied with either well-rotted compost or manure before planting would suit them best but this does not rule out the possibility of growing them successfully on a heavy soil provided the drainage is satisfactory.

Healthy stock

As black currants are subject to virus disease it is absolutely essential to start with healthy stock. I always opt for one-year-old plants covered by a Ministry of Agriculture's health certificate. This ensures that I start clean, free from big bud and reversion, which so often follows on after a big bud outbreak. Propagation of black currants is so easy that

Big bud condition

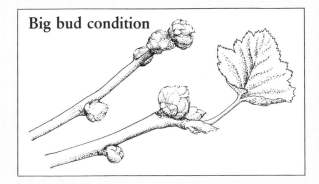

one could be tempted to accept cuttings from a neighbour or a friend but unless the parent bush is one hundred per cent healthy it is an unwise approach to black currant growing.

The big bud mite causes the buds to swell without opening or developing shoots. The mites move from bush to bush spreading a virus which causes reversion—a degenerate condition in which the leaves become smaller and nettle like. When this happens fruiting virtually ceases and there is no remedy.

Propagation

Always ensure cuttings come from healthy stock plants. Hard-wood cuttings are taken in the autumn. They should be about 23cm (9in) long, consisting of the current season's growth with the soft top 5cm (2in) removed. The cuttings, with all the buds intact, should be inserted into a trench for transplanting the following November or positioned directly in their cropping positions. In either case, firm the soil around the cutting and have at least half the cutting below ground.

Planting

It pays to prepare the ground thoroughly well ahead of planting time, which for me is November. A common mistake is overcrowding which lowers the black currants' cropping potential and makes the picking more awkward. The spacing I prefer is 1.5m (5ft) between plants and 2.2m (7ft) between the rows; by the time the second season arrives this is none too generous.

Taking black currant cuttings

Right: trim cuttings to about 23cm (9in) long
Below: make a slit trench with a spade and insert cuttings 15cm (6in) apart. Firm them in well

Pruning an established black currant bush

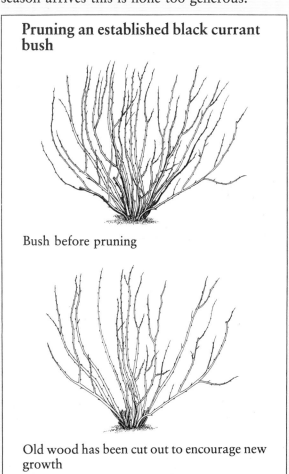

Bush before pruning

Old wood has been cut out to encourage new growth

In planting, make sure that the point at which the branches break above the roots is well below ground level; it is inadvisable to grow a black currant bush on a leg. Remember the usual points about spreading the fibrous roots out in the planting hole and firming the soil well around the young bush. Many gardeners shy at the recommendation to cut a newly-planted black currant bush down to two buds the following March as this means removing all the fruiting wood and leaving only about 5 cm (2in) of each branch above ground level. However it is this seemingly drastic operation that ensures good healthy cropping for years to come; without it the bush is likely to be a weak one for life.

Feeding
With the first pruning done it is time to give the first feed, which for me would be an organically-based fertiliser such as Back to Nature or fish, blood and bone, Growmore would also be suitable, at the rate of not less than 120g per sq m (4oz per sq yd). If midway through the growing season (July) the new growth is lacking in vigour a quick-acting liquid fertiliser based on urea, well watered in, would be a good growth stimulant.

For established bushes, late February or early March is the best time to apply the annual balanced fertiliser feed, the spring rains then wash it in just at the time it is most needed.

Pruning
Strong young growth is greatly encouraged by cutting out as much old wood as possible immediately after fruiting, leaving the current season's growths evenly distributed to form a shapely plant for fruiting the following year. Actually I find it easier to prune first and then pick the black currants off the cut branches.

Pests and Diseases

Sucking insects, such as aphids and capsids, are the chief pests of black currants. Aphids suck the sap and cause the leaves to pucker with red coloured blisters. Capsid attacks are

Recommended varieties of bush fruit: White Versailles (white currant), Red Lake (red currant), Wellington XXX (black currant) and Careless (gooseberry)

followed by brown spots on the leaves and result in a considerable check to leaf-growth. Spray immediately the attack is detected with a systemic greenfly killer to deal with both problems.

Big bud mite can be controlled with lime sulphur applied when the leaves are the size of a ten pence piece. It is reasonably effective but some varieties are sulphur shy and are liable to spray damage, Baldwin being a notable exception. As lime sulphur can be difficult to obtain, I would suggest hand picking and destruction of the swollen buds as soon as they are seen.

Varieties

Baldwin: compact growth habit and reliable cropping; has the highest vitamin C content. Season: late.

Boskoop Giant: a vigorous grower, makes a spreading bush, very large berries, fairly sweet. Season: early.

Laxton's Giant: a vigorous grower, spreading habit, large juicy berries but rather acid. Season: early.

Jet: a new variety, late flowering so less liable to frost damage, has a flavour of its own. Season: late.

Wellington XXX: a vigorous grower with a spreading habit, medium-sized berries, good flavour. Mid-season.

Red and White Currants

Both of these crop on old wood, consequently the pruning is different from that recommended for black currants. When grown as bushes, pruning should be done in the autumn with a view to retaining a sufficient number of main branches on which the laterals are shortened to about 5cm (2in). Both red and white currants require less nitrogen than black currants but the same fertilisers are suitable. However they should be applied at the rate of 100g per sq m (3oz per sq yd) in late February. The ripening berries must be protected with netting against birds.

Varieties

Laxton's No 1: a strong upright grower, good cropper, large bright red berries, good flavour. Season: early.

Red Lake: a good grower, upright habit, large red berries, good flavour. Season is a little later than Laxton's No 1.

White Versailles: crops well, the best white variety, medium to large berries of good flavour. Season: early.

Gooseberries

Because they are so easy to grow this fruit is often neglected in the garden, with the result that yields and quality suffer greatly. Some consideration of their needs will more than repay. An annual February application of Growmore fertiliser applied at the rate of 100g per sq m (3oz per sq yd) will ensure good growth and cropping. A deep soil with good drainage suits them best but they will grow well on practically any type of soil, provided the drainage is satisfactory.

Planting

On poor, light or gravelly soils it is wise to improve the fertility and moisture-holding capacity of the soil before planting by digging in some well-rotted compost or manure. As gooseberries are always susceptible to a potash deficiency in any soil it is a good idea

Pruning a red currant bush

Established bush before pruning; note well-developed leg

Leaders have been tipped back and laterals shortened to 5cm (2in)

to apply some sulphate of potash at the rate of 60g per sq m (2oz per sq yd) at the very start. A brown marginal leaf scorch indicates the deficiency but once it shows up it may take two seasons to correct during which time the cropping results will suffer.

As with other bush fruits the best planting time is November with the ground having been prepared several weeks ahead. I plant one-year-old bushes; no time is saved by purchasing older and usually more expensive plants. Unlike black currants, the plants should have been grown on a clean leg with the lowest branch at least 15cm (6in) above ground level. Without this leg, picking and weeding underneath the bushes can be a painful business. To allow space not only for the bushes to develop but also for picking, I plant at least 1.5m (5ft) apart in a row.

Pruning

The branches of newly-planted bushes should be cut back in March to about 8cm (3in). This means no fruit in the first season. Established bushes can be pruned after fruiting or, better still, in February. In districts where bullfinches are a problem, complete overall netting prevents loss of buds. Pruning consists of forming an open system of main branches with the side laterals cut back to about 5cm (2in).

Gooseberry sawfly caterpillar

This pest can reduce gooseberry foliage to shreds

Propagation

Propagation is easy. Take cuttings of new mature wood in late August, choosing strong new growth. Remove all but the top six buds

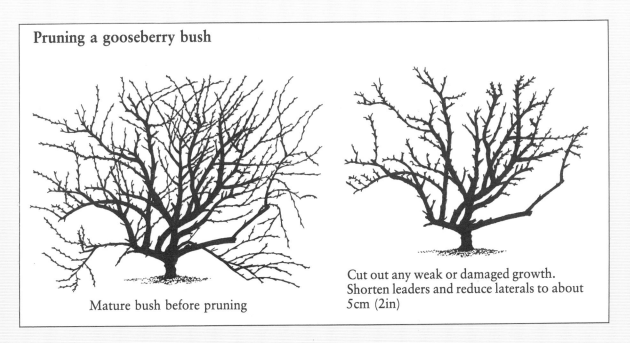

Pruning a gooseberry bush

Mature bush before pruning

Cut out any weak or damaged growth. Shorten leaders and reduce laterals to about 5cm (2in)

and insert them 30cm (12in) apart into a slit trench made with a spade. The following summer you will have one-year-old bushes on a good clean leg for planting out in their permanent position.

Pests and Diseases
Gooseberry sawfly larvae, which given half a chance eat the leaves to skeletons, can be controlled with a derris insecticide. Gooseberry mildew, seen first in the growing tip which begins to appear white and powdery, can be checked by spraying with benlate.

Varieties
Careless: the most popular variety, large green berries, cook well when still small, good flavour when ripe.
Golden Drop: a small yellow berry, rich flavour, subject to mildew.
Leveller: a weak grower on poor soils, large yellow berries, excellent flavour.
Whitesmith: an upright grower, large yellow-green berries, good flavour.
Whinham's Industry: an upright grower, has dark red berries, good flavour when ripe. Does well on heavy soils.

Strawberries

There are few districts in the country where strawberries are not a practical gardening proposition. All that is needed is some careful consideration regarding the selection of the growing site coupled with thorough preparation of the soil before planting.

Strawberries succeed best in full sun; varying degrees of shade result in less fruit and weak foliage. The more traditional summer-fruiting varieties blossom in May and the flowers are very susceptible to frost damage, so with cold frosty air flowing downhill like water it is wise to plant if possible on the highest ground within the garden.

Preparing the ground
Strawberries need a rich, well-drained soil and, apart from the chalky types, most kinds can be bolstered up to suit them. At no time during the growing season should they go

Removing strawberry runners

short of water and the best insurance against this is to incorporate liberal amounts of well-rotted compost or manure before planting.

The ground should be dug to a good spade's depth at least a month ahead of planting to allow time for the soil to settle. On soils of low fertility a post-digging application of fish, blood and bone fertiliser or Growmore applied at the rate of 100g per sq m (3oz per sq yd) will improve matters. The area selected should be cleared of perennial weed roots, otherwise a permanent weed problem capable of swamping the strawberries will soon develop.

When to plant
The best time for planting strawberries is late August or September, provided that in the event of dry weather they are watered regularly. Early planting plus the warmer soil and good growing conditions enables stronger roots and fat crowns to develop before the winter. The great advantage gained from a September planting comes in the first season. The plants, then termed 'maidens', crop without any harm; not only are the berries larger but they are also slightly earlier than those produced on older plants. In fact first year results are often so good that many gardeners and commercial growers rely entirely on first season cropping and replant each September on fresh ground.

Opposite: Gento **Inset:** Cambridge Favourite

104

Early spring plantings are easier, the soil is then usually well supplied with moisture and plants as a rule are more readily available and cheaper. Summer-fruiting varieties planted in March or early April should have all their blossom removed that season to allow them time to establish in readiness for the fruiting season the following June. Varieties which fruit in September and October will be strong enough by that time to carry a crop so blossom removal will not be necessary.

Planting

Plants covered by a Ministry of Agriculture Certificate of Health are the best buy. These carry a clean bill of health which can only be ensured when parent plants are healthy, grown in isolation and kept absolutely free of sucking insects such as greenfly which spread disease around. Plant health is of prime importance and strawberries degenerate rapidly when infected with virus disease, therefore it is risky to accept rooted plants lifted from a cropping strawberry bed.

Planting should be done carefully, if the roots are at all dry give them a soaking in cold water for a few minutes. Allow 38cm (15in) between the plants in the row and 75cm (30in) between rows. Closer planting results in lower yields per plant and problems during the growing season especially at picking time.

Bare-rooted plants should be planted with their roots well spread out, but plants supplied in small net pots with protruding roots should be planted complete without disturbance. It is important to plant firmly but on no account should the crown of the plant be below the soil surface. Ideally it should be just at ground level. Plants with their crowns well above ground level never do too well, for this reason I always check autumn-planted strawberries the following spring as frosts have a tendency to lift them. If this has happened I firm them back into place with my hands.

Feeding

For August and September plantings and established beds, late February or early March is about the best time to apply a feed. For strawberries I prefer organically-based fertilisers such as Back to Nature or fish, blood and bone fertiliser applied at the rate of 100g per sq m (3oz per sq yd). This early application gets down to the roots in time to help at the commencement of the growing season. It encourages strength in the crown development from which the flower trusses emerge and subsequently helps to give good sized berries. In addition it will keep the plants in good health.

A repeat application after fruiting makes sure that the plants are going to be fit and strong for a second season's cropping. With good management there is no reason why a bed that starts healthy should not carry on for three or four fruiting seasons, although with the passing of time the fruit will be slightly smaller. An early-spring planting should have a similar feed in June or early July, again 100g per sq m (3oz per sq yd) would be the average application rate.

At no time should weeds be allowed to establish themselves as competitors for moisture, nutrients and light, for this would have a serious effect on crop yields. Frequent use of the Dutch hoe whilst the weeds are small is the answer, as this surface cultivation can be done without damaging the strawberry roots.

Clean fruit

When fruit setting commences, covering the ground under the trusses prevents heavy rains splashing soil on the fruit. Barley straw was the traditional covering but now thin perforated black plastic sheeting is more generally used, the plants being eased through slits. Do not lay this cover down too early as the risk of frost damage to the open blossom is increased.

At fruiting time the plants start to produce runners in quantity which if left will root in masses around the parent plants. Unless the runners are needed for producing a batch of new plants it is best to remove them at an early stage. It may prove to be a weekly job for over a month. I use a knife or a pair of scissors for the job as pulling them off often results in the removal of part of the parent plant.

Propagation

Home production of plants is only worthwhile if the parent plants are one hundred per cent healthy, with large leaves

Propagating strawberries

Plunge a 9-cm (3½-in) pot filled with potting compost into the soil and peg down a runner with bent pieces of wire

free from mottling, crinkling or distortion of any sort which could suggest virus. From really strong plants selected runners can be pegged down with a hair-pin-shaped piece of wire into a sunken 9-cm (3½-in) pot filled with John Innes potting compost No. 2. If the compost is kept moist a runner will quickly root. As soon as this happens the extension of the runner beyond the pot should be cut off, but the link with the parent plant retained until the new plant is required for planting out.

An early crop
Established plants out of doors covered with cloches early in March will ripen a month ahead of the same variety left unprotected. Remember these cloched plants will need watering. As the season progresses the cloches should be spaced a little apart for ventilation and uncovered on a fine day to allow the bees unhindered access to pollinate.

With a greenhouse available strawberries in April are possible. To obtain this early crop put young well-rooted plants into 13-cm (5-in) pots in September. Keep them in good condition out of doors until February, then bring them inside after a thorough spraying against greenfly and give them a liquid feed to get them started into growth.

Pests and diseases
Greenfly can spread virus, spray with systemic greenfly killer before an infestation develops. Caterpillars chew the foliage lessening the vigour of the plants. Spray with derris insecticide. Slugs and snails attack the fruit, the answer is to scatter slug pellets around the plants. Botrytis (grey mould) and mildew develop on ripening fruit, spray with benomyl at blossom time and repeat. The major pests of the fruits are birds for which overall netting of the crop is the only answer.

Varieties
Summer fruiting
Cambridge Favourite: the most popular variety, vigorous grower, heavy cropper, fair flavour.
Domanil: a late mid-season variety, heavy cropper, good flavour.
Gorella: vigorous grower, upright habit.
Grandee: early, very large berries, fair flavour.
Royal Sovereign: not easy to grow and very susceptible to virus diseases but it is the best flavoured strawberry.
Tamella: the best substitute for Royal Sovereign; a good cropper of excellent flavour.
Autumn fruiting
Gento: fair cropper, produces few runners, very good flavour.
Rabunda: vigorous grower, heavy cropper.

Netting strawberries
As with other fruit crops, netting is the only real answer to the bird problem

TENDER FRUITS

Although apricots, peaches and nectarines are winter hardy their blossom and the young fruitlets that follow are very susceptible to frost damage. Figs are not completely hardy and need some protection in winter when grown outside; the developing fruitlets are also very liable to damage by frost. All four need some form of protection to ensure worthwhile cropping. The degree of protection varies but the nearer their micro-climates are to that of the Mediterranean region, the more dependable the results are likely to be.

Protection from frost

All these crops can be grown with success in a greenhouse especially if some heat is available early in the season, although this is not absolutely essential. An advantage of growing peaches and nectarines indoors is that they do not suffer from peach leaf curl, a disease which can be such a plague on trees grown outdoors.

Peaches, nectarines and apricots blossom very early. Apricots lead the way in February and are soon followed by peaches and nectarines in March. Frost damage at blossom time out of doors is a high risk and even continuous cold weather without a frost can result in a poor fruit set. In the greenhouse the midday temperatures at blossom time are usually high enough to produce viable pollen, which in the absence of bees should be transferred from flower to flower using a soft camel hair brush.

Growing conditions

Good light for peaches and nectarines is just as important as protection against the inclement weather. Therefore it is essential that the greenhouse roof and side glass is kept clean, especially in the early part of the growing season. Plastic-covered greenhouses afford less protection against frost and let in less light than those fitted with glass.

Whilst a greenhouse can improve the climatic conditions it also increases the chances of pest problems, especially red spider mite infestations, unless the day to day management is planned on a preventive basis. Red spider mite thrives when the atmosphere and growing conditions are dry, which means that the trees should never suffer from dryness at the roots, nor should the air be allowed to become excessively dry. To avoid this happening I make a habit of watering the centre path in the greenhouse once or twice on hot days and closing the door afterwards to build up the humidity in the air.

One point to bear in mind, fan-trained trees do restrict light within a greenhouse used for growing a variety of plants. So always plant such a tree on the north side to allow maximum light for other plants. The actual cultivation and training is virtually the same for trees grown in the greenhouse and outdoors, except, of course, that under glass the fruit ripens much earlier and is somewhat larger and generally of a higher quality.

Apricots

Apricots are the earliest-blossoming fruit in this country. Even outdoors it is usually in full bloom before the end of February, which means that it can only be cropped without protection in the most favourable districts such as the south-west.

Even so it must be covered at night with old curtain material or something similar to give protection against frost damage. So as far as growing this fruit out of doors goes, what follows is for the favoured gardeners in the south-west who may have a south-facing wall about 4m (13ft) high or those who have a suitable greenhouse.

Even with the protection of a greenhouse apricots can still be difficult. Temperatures above 7.5°C (45°F) before the fruitlets stone lead to trouble and even when that stage is past, temperatures in excess of 16°C (60°F) can cause fruit drop.

The soil

Apricots are not too fussy about soil type provided it is well drained; if it is inclined to be calcareous so much the better. Some free lime will be needed in the soil when cropping starts as calcium is essential for the formation of stones, without it the young fruitlets fail to stay on the tree. If the soil is at all inclined to be acid, garden lime applied at the rate of 120g per sq m (4oz per sq yd) and worked in before planting will be a wise precaution.

Planting

Late October or November is the best time for planting. Start with a fan-trained tree, one that has already been partially trained in the nursery. My advice is to go for a two-year-old tree. It is best to plant an apricot so the base of its stem is a few inches in front of the wall, fence or greenhouse side. Make sure that the hole is large enough to accommodate all the roots without cramping. A handful of bonemeal scattered around before filling in with fine soil helps root development. Cut off cleanly any jagged root ends that may be present.

As with all trees planted against a wall, fence or in the greenhouse border drying out of the soil must be guarded against at all times. After planting in a greenhouse watering may be necessary immediately.

Pruning and training

Horizontal training wires will be required. These should be spaced 30cm (12in) apart and held at least 5cm (2in) in front of the back support which should be at least 2m (6ft) high. When the tree breaks into growth the process of building up the fan of young branches begins. This involves disbudding, pinching out young unwanted shoots and stopping the growth of the main branches of the fan as necessary. This should be carried out as early in the growing season as possible. The unwanted young growths are those that either grow downwards, directly outwards or back towards the supporting wall. The shoots which develop from the upper sides of the branches are the ones to look out for and tie

in loosely to the wires. In this way the tree rapidly develops with the branches evenly spaced within the fan.

Pests and diseases

Fortunately apricots are not very much subject to pests and diseases. Greenfly and caterpillars are occasionally a problem. These can be dealt with by spraying with a mixed insecticide based on HCH and dimethoate.

Varieties

I have tried Farmingdale and Alfred. Both these varieties produce good quality, well-flavoured fruit.

Below: The chances of a good crop of apricots are greatly increased by growing under glass

Peaches and Nectarines

The difference between the fruits of peaches and nectarines is seen mainly in the skin. Whereas that of a peach is something akin to fine velvet, the skin of a nectarine is smooth. In addition a well-grown ripe nectarine has a finer flesh texture and a somewhat fuller flavour, but the growing techniques are identical for both.

Protection

These fruits are winter hardy in this country but with blossom time sometimes as early as late February, protection against possible spring frost damage is essential, expecially for trees grown outside. From fruit set to the ripe-fruit stage, warm protected growing conditions are needed all the time. An unheated greenhouse goes much of the way to providing better protected climatic conditions, but my own experience in Worcestershire has taught me that it is advisable to have some form of heating to prevent night temperatures falling below freezing point, from mid-February onwards.

A south- or west-facing wall or fence gives the trees considerable protection and provides that extra warmth during the growing season which makes all the difference. Only in the south-eastern parts of the country, where summers are usually warm, should the planting of free-standing trees be considered. Fan-trained trees are the best proposition for planting both under glass and outside, a two-year-old tree with the training already started in the nursery is the best buy.

Preparing the site

Controlling the growth starts with the preparation of the planting area. It used to be common practice to dig out the greenhouse border to a depth of 1m (3ft) and then make a compacted 15-cm (6-in) thick foundation of chalk with some rubble for drainage about it. This did much to prevent the rampant growth which sometimes develops in established trees.

A good growing medium is a heavy loam made up from old well-rotted turf with some old mortar rubble mixed in with it, but both may be difficult to get nowadays. Recently I have had to settle for a thorough cultivation of the site soil plus a liberal application of garden lime at least 120g per sq m (4oz per sq yd) worked in at the same time. Peaches and nectarines always need lime in the soil, not only for their general health but also for supplying the essential calcium needed during the fruit-stoning period.

Before planting, the horizontal support wires should be put in position. I like to have the wires 25cm (10in) apart and in the greenhouse carried up to the eaves to give maximum cropping area. Each fan-trained tree will need at least a 4-m (12-ft) run for training; 2m (about 6ft) on either side of the centre.

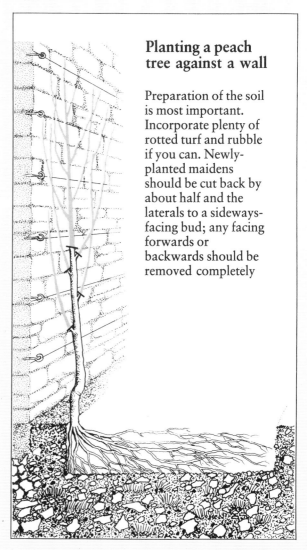

Planting a peach tree against a wall

Preparation of the soil is most important. Incorporate plenty of rotted turf and rubble if you can. Newly-planted maidens should be cut back by about half and the laterals to a sideways-facing bud; any facing forwards or backwards should be removed completely

110

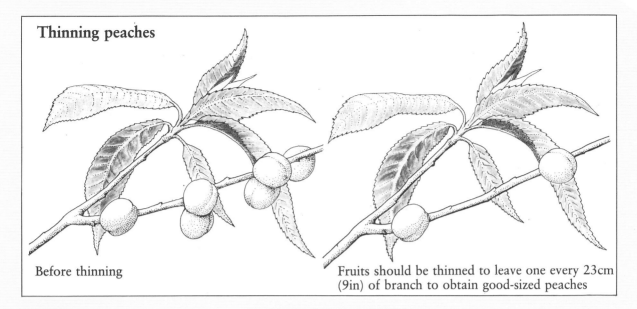

Thinning peaches

Before thinning

Fruits should be thinned to leave one every 23cm (9in) of branch to obtain good-sized peaches

Planting

The best time for planting is late October or November. Remember to plant firmly at the same depth as the tree was growing in the nursery (the depth mark will be clearly seen on the stem). Tie in branches with raffia to the wires, not too tightly so there is ample room for the branches to expand within the ties. As peach leaf curl is so prevalent it is wise to spray all newly-planted dormant trees immediately with a liquid copper fungicide.

Pruning and training

When the leaf buds break it is time to commence training. This is basically the same as for apricots. The developing buds breaking downwards, inwards and outwards are rubbed out whilst still small with finger and thumb. The aim at all times being to distribute the upward growing young shoots evenly within the expanding fan, leaving ultimately at least 8cm (5in) between each shoot for fruiting the following season. Any extra strong upward growing shoots emerging from the centre should be cut out without delay for a fan with a slight 'V' in the centre is an advantage. It is not wise to allow trees to fruit in the first season.

When fruiting does commence the young peaches or nectarines may need thinning. Thin to about 25cm (10in) apart on the branches and the fruit will be larger. Any leaves overshadowing the fruit should be removed or tucked in behind to prevent a shadow effect on the skin. An application of Growmore fertiliser applied at the rate of 60 to 100g per sq m (2 to 3oz per sq yd) in February keeps the trees in good condition.

Pests and diseases

Pests include aphids and red spider mite, against which apply malathion according to the manufacturer's instructions. Dryness at the roots and in the air increases the red spider mite problem on trees grown indoors. By regular watering and damping down the greenhouse path, the atmosphere is kept humid and the pest deterred. Whilst the trees are completely dormant an application of tar oil winter wash, such as Mortegg, at the strength recommended by the manufacturer will destroy aphid eggs and so make greenfly

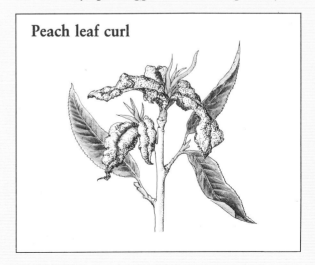

Peach leaf curl

control the following season much easier.

Peach leaf curl is the main disease affecting peaches and nectarines. After the initial copper fungicide application after planting all trees it will not be necessary to repeat the application on trees grown indoors. However on outdoor trees repeat applications after leaf fall (November) and at bud break (February or early March) is virtually a must every year.

Varieties
Peaches
Peregrine: the most reliable variety, August, excellent flavour.
Rochester: crops well, August, fair flavour.
Duke of York: large fruit, July, excellent flavour.

Nectarines
Early Rivers: large fruit, July, excellent flavour.

Figs

Figs are very easy to grow but far more difficult to crop consistently due to the variable climate of this country.

Growing under cover
In a greenhouse it is possible to provide suitable climatic conditions for two or even three fruit crops in a single season but this involves heating and growth control. With space and heating at a premium it is wise to plant the tree in a very large pot or other container, using some old turf-stack loam with lime or old mortar rubble mixed in with it. Firm planting is needed and re-potting with the minimum of root disturbance would be needed every other year. The size of the pot will restrict growth and thus induce fruiting.

Regular watering throughout the growing season is important and an occasional liquid fertiliser feed will be required to keep the plant healthy. The tree, if growing in a pot could be stood outside during the growing season and taken in to enjoy the protection of the greenhouse during the winter.

Growing outside
A fig growing out of doors should be firmly

planted in some form of large container to prevent excessive wood growth and induce fruiting. However, ensure whatever container the roots are restricted in has adequate drainage holes. It should also have winter protection, especially against frost; dry bracken makes an effective covering.

Varieties
Brown Turkey: the most suitable variety for growing in this country.

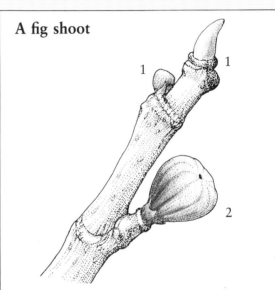

A fig shoot

At the tip of the shoot, above the ripening figs, can be seen next year's embryo fruits (1) and those partially developed (2) which will be killed by frost

Restricting the root run

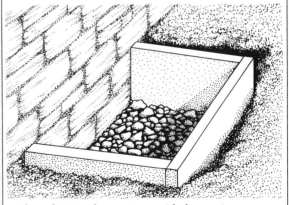

Plant figs in a large strong sided container or a hole lined with concrete slabs to encourage fruit production

Opposite: Figs can crop well after a good summer

Frame Melons

The present day costs of heating a greenhouse to maintain the necessary early season day temperature of 18.5 to 21°C (65 to 70°F) and night temperature not lower than 16°C (60°F) has all but eliminated heated indoor melon growing as we knew it years ago. However the recent introduction of F_1-hybrid varieties capable of growing and cropping in lower temperature regimes has resulted in melons being grown successfully in cold frames, unheated greenhouses and even outside under cloches in the warmer districts.

Even so it must be appreciated that the degree of success varies from season to season, the best results are always more likely to occur in the southern half of the country. Seasons which start off with a warm spring and then go into a sunny summer suit melons best, for then it is just a question of making the most of the available warmth and sunshine.

Raising the plants

Heat is needed to germinate the seed, so in a cold greenhouse I use an economical electrically-heated propagating frame, fitted with a thermostat which is set to maintain a constant temperature of 18.5 to 21°C (65 to 70°F). Using a peat-based seed compost I sow the seed singly, on edge, in small peat pots which have been previously watered whilst still empty. After sowing the compost is watered.

Germination will take just a few days. As soon as the seedlings begin to show their first true leaves I pot them on into 9-cm (3½-in) pots, this time using a peat-based potting compost. From this stage onwards the plants grow well, provided the temperature stays around 16°C (60°F), and the quality of daylight is relatively good.

If you are not fortunate enough to own a greenhouse maybe your kitchen windowsill is light enough and has daytime temperatures suitable to meet these requirements. If this is the case it may only be necessary to move the

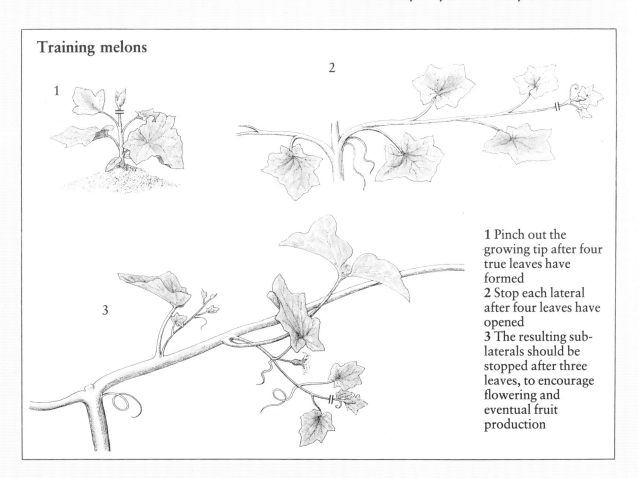

Training melons

1

2

3

1 Pinch out the growing tip after four true leaves have formed
2 Stop each lateral after four leaves have opened
3 The resulting sub-laterals should be stopped after three leaves, to encourage flowering and eventual fruit production

Pollinating a melon flower

Use a soft paint brush to apply the pollen; note the embryo fruit behind the female flower

pots at night to the middle of the room, away from the night-time chill.

Planting

I have found by experience that planting out into unheated conditions before the end of May is unwise because night temperatures are still low. If the plants suffer a severe cold check at this critical stage, they seldom really recover.

There is still nothing better for growing melons than a mound of old stacked turf with a sprinkling of garden lime on it; for unlike cucumbers, melons should not be grown in an over-rich medium. A mound of thoroughly-rotted garden compost grows good melons without excessive foliage growth. In recent years I have been using peat growing bags with two plants in each bag. I line the bags up at the higher end of the frame, a bag being just about the width of a standard frame light.

Whatever the growing medium, the young melon plants should be planted on a slight mound so that water does not collect around the stem. Careful watering is a golden rule for successful melon growing.

Training

When the second set of true leaves has formed pinch out the growing tip, this allows two laterals to develop. These in turn are pinched back to four leaves. The sub-laterals which subsequently develop are then stopped at the third leaf. It is on these sub-laterals that the female flowers develop, which subsequently develop into fruit.

Pollination

I try to wait till a plant has five or six female flowers before attempting pollination. Then when the temperature is at its highest at midday, I gently touch the centres of one or two male flowers with a soft camel hair brush to collect pollen. This is very gently transferred to the stigmas of wide-open female flowers. To tell the difference between male and female flowers look behind the petals; the female flowers have a small bulbous swelling, whereas in the male flowers this is absent. Under frame conditions I aim at four melons per plant, ideally pollinated at the same time otherwise the melons are likely to be uneven sizes. I choose the four largest young fruits and remove the rest.

General care

During the growing season I give a fortnightly feed with a tomato fertiliser applied according to the manufacturer's instructions. Be careful

The variety Charantais grows well in this country

not to overfeed as this will produce foliage at the expense of fruit set. In very hot sunny weather I shade the glass to prevent scorching and at the same time increase the ventilation. As ripening time gets near the watering should be considerably reduced to avoid cracking of the fruit; the warning that this stage has come is a slight aroma apparent when opening the frame.

Varieties
Charantais: orange flesh, delicious flavour.
Ogen: green flesh, needs a long warm summer to build up its full flavour.
Sweetheart: an F_1 hybrid with scarlet flesh, excellent flavour.

Grapes

Present day fuel costs virtually rule out thoughts that we gardeners might have of growing grape vines in the traditional way in a heated greenhouse. So having myself abandoned any such hope I feel that in this instance I should deal with growing grapes in an unheated greenhouse or in a sheltered position outside. In either case the consideration must be the question of space. To get the best results a vine should have at least 1.5m (5ft) of space. In a small greenhouse this may mean that nearly the whole of one side is devoted to it. Another point to remember is that a vine is a very rapid producer of new growth and unless the routine pruning operations are carried out at the correct times, a greenhouse can quickly become a jungle of lush leaf growth, with little prospect of fruit. In other words a neglectful gardener should not start dessert grape growing indoors.

The protection afforded by an unheated greenhouse can provide a climate in the growing season akin to that in the Mediterranean region, which is the grapes' native habitat. So, by careful management, it is possible to grow good quality dessert grapes in practically all districts. However, out of doors the real chances of success are restricted to the warmer southern areas of the country, but even there a sunny wall is needed for extra daylight background heating.

Preparing the soil
Whichever way they are grown, so much depends on the soil and the thoroughness of the planting preparation. The soil must be well drained otherwise root dieback will occur when it becomes waterlogged. Vines thrive on fertile soil and years ago it was common practice to bury a dead animal, even as large as a cow, deep down below the chosen planting site. Nowadays we must rely on an organic fertiliser such as fish, blood and bone, a liberal application of up to 230g per sq m (8oz per sq yd) would not be too much. In addition some well-rotted manure or compost worked into the border at the same time would be all to the good.

Planting
When greenhouses were built on brick foundations vines in heated greenhouses were planted inside the borders. However for growing in a cold greenhouse they were planted outside, with the rod (the mainstem) brought into the house through a hole in the wall. The modern greenhouse has little or no foundations, and so I always plant in the border, it makes feeding easier and watering somewhat more controllable.

Young vines are usually sold as pot-grown plants, consequently it is possible to plant at any time of the year; but all the same October and November are the best months for the job. Before you start planting a vine, make sure that the young stem will finally be at least 45cm (18in) in front of the greenhouse wall. It is at this stage that a scattering of garden lime, 230g per sq m (8oz per sq yd) over the whole border area, is needed.

Care should be taken not to plant too deeply. If the plant is dormant, the roots can be well spread out within the planting hole. Fill in with fine soil around the stem, making sure that at the finish the potting-compost-level mark on the stem is just above new soil level. The border soil should be kept moist during the winter.

Pruning and training
In the spring young shoots will develop and as I prefer greenhouse vines with two rods, I select two of the strongest growths for training. I then pinch out the growing tips of those shoots not required after they have

reached the five- or six-leaf stage. For training and support horizontal wiring is needed. Spacing of the wires should be about 30cm (12in) ranged up the side and along the roof of the greenhouse. This wiring should be fixed a few inches in front of the glass (the same applies when the vines are to be grown in front of a wall).

Tying in the selected young shoots commences immediately. In my case with two rods per plant in mind, they start first growing out horizontally in opposite directions. Then when they are about 1.5m (5ft) apart, the training upwards begins. The idea being that ultimately all fruit on the laterals will have, if need be, 75cm (30in) of horizontal wiring for cropping. Two-rod vines can be planted 3m (10ft) apart, but if vines are grown as single

Pruning a vine

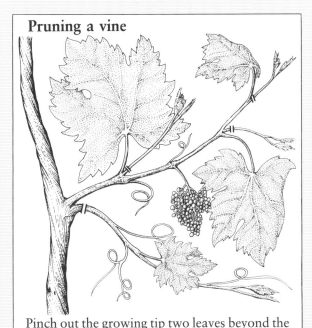

Pinch out the growing tip two leaves beyond the flower truss. Remove any sub-laterals

rods the distance could be only 1.5m (5ft).

During the first growing season the young rods may make 2m (6ft) of growth. All the developing side shoots (sub-laterals) should be pinched back to one leaf. At the end of the first season, when the leaves have fallen in November, the rods should be cut back to one third of their length. At the end of the second year the rods are cut back to two thirds of their end-of-season length. In subsequent years it is just a matter of containing the growth within the available space. One

golden rule is never cut back into old wood during the growing season or when the sap is rising, otherwise non-stop bleeding will occur. Therefore always cut back old wood during dormancy, immediately after leaf fall in November. After bud break, lateral growths develop rapidly and usually in excessive numbers, only one is needed on each side of a rod at each horizontal wire position.

After selecting and tying in the laterals I wait a few days before removing the unwanted extra laterals, just in case any of those tied in wilt as a result of damage. As soon as the first flower truss appears on a lateral I pinch out the growing tip at two leaves beyond the flower truss. From then on all the subsequent sub-lateral growths are removed at the earliest possible stage. Only by keeping completely on top of this early-season growth is it possible to prevent a jungle situation developing.

The fruit

Watering and feeding is needed during the growing season, I give them a monthly feed of liquid fertiliser. It is wise to strictly limit the cropping of a young vine. In the second season it will produce flower trusses and fruit; two or three bunches at the most should be its quota. You can perhaps allow double that number in the third season and from then on it will reach full cropping, but even so over-cropping will result in small berries.

Thinning of the bunches should be done early using a pair of sharp pointed scissors. It is time consuming but done well results in

Thinning the bunch

Thin out young fruits using a pair of sharp pointed scissors and a piece of wood to avoid marking the berries. This will result in larger grapes and better-shaped bunches

Opposite: Grapes trained up under the greenhouse roof. **Inset:** Black Hamburg

Above: In favoured areas a good crop of grapes for wine making can be produced outside

better shaped bunches and larger berries. During June, July and possibly August some shading of the greenhouse may be needed to prevent leaf scorch of the foliage close to the roof glass.

Good ventilation reduces the risk of mildew but if it does appear on the foliage or fruit spray immediately with benomyl at the rates recommended by the manufacturer. Towards the end of the growing season, mid-August to September, a slight reduction in the ventilation will increase the overall greenhouse temperature and allow the sun to swell and ripen the grapes. Wait for a bunch to be fully mature before cutting. If cut with a piece of the lateral attached the bunch can be kept fresh by placing the stem in water.

Winter care
Finally at the end of the growing season when the rods are dormant, cut the laterals back to one or two eyes (buds) that are close to the rod. Then lower the rods down for the winter; this routine I find improves bud break in the spring, especially if during the winter the rods are subjected to frost by leaving the greenhouse door open. On old vines the rods may be covered with rough loose bark, this should be carefully rubbed off during the dormant season.

Outdoor vines
The treatment here discussed for indoor grapes is roughly the same recommended for outdoor vines. The only difference is that if grapes are grown for wine making on free-standing fences, the rods should be trained along horizontal wires but no higher than 1m (3ft).

Varieties
Having tried several varieties in unheated greenhouses I have come to the following conclusions:
Black Hamburg: this still remains the most reliable cropper, it is a good grower, not too fussy about soil conditions and it is certainly the best variety for planting outside.
Buckland Sweetwater: a white grape which has an excellent flavour, but in my experience needs heat to bring the best out of it.
Riesling-Sylvaner and Seyve-Villard: these are the best wine grape varieties I have grown. Both varieties are also suitable for dessert provided the weather is able to ripen the berries fully.

119

Pests and Diseases

Pest	Damage	Plants Affected	Treatment
Aphids	Sap sucked from leaves, which often curl up. Plant is weakened.	Most fruit. Serious pest of strawberries as they carry virus disease	On fruit trees, canefruit and currants spray with a tar oil winter wash during the dormant season (December-February) to destroy eggs. During the growing season spray all fruit with malathion or a systemic insecticide where it occurs.
Big bud mite	Buds become abnormally large but do not open. They are filled with mites which often spread reversion, a virus condition. Unfruitfulness results.	Black currants	Remove and burn infested buds. Spray with lime sulphur when leaves are the size of a 10 pence piece, repeat three weeks later. Remember some varieties of black currant are sulphur shy.
Capsid bug	On apple shows as brown spots on leaves and corky patches on fruit. On currants small brown holes puncture the leaves and the young shoots are crippled.	Apple, currants	Spray with a systemic insecticide or fenitrothion in apple at green bud stage and petal fall, on currants just before the flowers fully open and at fruit set.
Caterpillars	Foliage is eaten.	Apple, pear, plum, damson, cherry	Spray with a tar oil winter wash in the dormant season. Spray with fenitrothion when the young leaves open or at first sign of damage.
Codling moth	Maggoty apples.	Apples	Spray with fenitrothion at petal fall and repeat three times at fortnightly intervals. Tie corrugated cardboard bands as traps round the trunks in July. Remove and burn these before December.
Pear midge	Maggots feed in young fruitlets causing them to fall.	Pear	Spray with fenitrothion at white bud stage. Collect and burn fallen fruitlets.
Raspberry beetle	Eggs laid in the blossom results in maggoty fruits.	All cane fruits, especially raspberries	Spray raspberries with fenitrothion or liquid derris at white bud and petal fall. Other cane fruits should be sprayed just before or just after flowering and again two weeks later.
Red spider mite	Tiny mites feed on the under sides of the leaves causing them to turn brown and dry up. In severe cases webs may be visible.	Most fruit growing outside or in the greenhouse	Spray fruit outside with malathion or a systemic insecticide during the growing season. Keep plants watered and in dry weather and in the greenhouse spray the foliage with water. Keep the greenhouse atmosphere humid by damping down.

Pest	Damage	Plants Affected	Treatment
Sawfly	Maggots in apples cause a rough mark on the skin. Larvae can strip gooseberries of their foliage.	Apple, gooseberry	Spray apples with a systemic insecticide or fenitrothion at petal fall. Spray gooseberries with HCH, fenitrothion or liquid derris as soon as an attack is observed.
Scale	Sap sucking creatures which adhere tightly to the foliage.	Peaches, apricots and vines grown under glass	Spray with a systemic insecticide or malathion.
Suckers	Blossom turns brown and withers.	Apple, pear	Spray with a tar oil wash when trees are dormant. Spray with malathion or fenitrothion at green and pink bud stages.
Woolly aphid	Aphids with a waxed woolly covering. Attacks often provide opening for canker.	Apple	Paint infestations with methylated spirits using a stiff brush. Where pests are widespread spray with malathion or a systemic insecticide.

Disease	Damage	Plants Affected	Treatment
Botrytis (grey mould)	Grey mould attacks first during cold, wet weather. Berries rot completely.	Strawberries	Spray with benomyl or captan as the first flowers open. Repeat every 10 days. Keep plants clean by removing dead leaves.
Canker	Swollen rough and ragged growths on branches, often circular or elliptical.	Apple, can also attack pear	Scrape the canker away and treat the cleaned area with wound paint. Spray with a copper fungicide when the leaves fall in autumn.
Mildew	Young shoots are crippled by this fungus which appears white on the bark surface. Attacks fruit of vines and gooseberries.	Apples, vines, gooseberry	Spray apples at pink bud stage and vines with a systemic fungicide or dinocap. Dinocap smoke can be used in the greenhouse. Spray gooseberries at the first sign of American gooseberry mildew and repeat at fortnightly intervals.
Peach leaf curl	Leaves curl and red blisters form on them. They drop prematurely.	Peaches and nectarines growing outdoors	Spray with a liquid copper fungicide in November and again just as growth begins in February or early March.
Scab	Dark sunken patches on the fruit. Sooty marks can also occur on the leaves. Common in clean-air areas.	Apple, pear	Spray with captan at bud burst. Repeat at green bud, white or pink bud petal fall and at least twice as the young fruitlets swell.
Silver leaf	Young foliage becomes silvery followed by decline in vigour and cropping of the tree.	Plums, damsons	Cut out and burn infected wood immediately. Grub up and burn badly diseased trees.
Storage rots	Deterioration and rotting of flesh when fruits are stored.	Apple	Spray fruits with captan in August and before harvesting.

Useful addresses

Seed houses
Asmer Seeds Ltd, Asmer House, Ash Street, Leicester
Samuel Dobie & Son Ltd, Upper Dee Mills, Llangollen, Clwyd
Hurst, Gunson, Cooper Taber Ltd, Witham, Essex
Sutton & Sons Ltd, Hele Road, Torquay, Devon
W. J. Unwin Ltd, Histon, Cambridge

Potatoes
Donald Maclean, Dornock Farm, Crieff, Perthshire

Fruit
Blackmoor Nurseries, Liss, Hampshire
Hillier & Sons, Winchester, Hampshire
Ken Muir, Honeypot Farm, Weeley Heath, Clacton-on-Sea, Essex
Thomas Rivers & Son Ltd, The Nurseries, Sawbridgemouth, Hertfordshire
Scotts Nurseries (Merriott) Ltd, Merriott, Somerset

Herbs
J. & B. Hugo, Ashfields Herb Nursery, Hinstock, Market Drayton
The Old Rectory Herb Garden, Ightham, Kent
Tumblers Bottom Herb Farm, Kilmersdon, Radstock

Fruit cages
Agriframes Ltd, Charlwoods Road, East Grinstead, Sussex

Greenhouses and frames
Alitex Ltd, Station Road, Alton, Hampshire
Alton Glasshouses Ltd, P.O. Box 3, Bewdley, Worcestershire
Crittall Warmlife Ltd, Crittall Road, Witham, Essex
Edenlite Ltd, Hawksworth, Swindon, Wiltshire
Kenkast Buildings Ltd, Astley, Manchester
Marley Greenhouses Ltd, Storrington, Sussex

Societies
The Royal Horticultural Society, Vincent Square, London SW1P 2PE
Membership of this society gives free access to the Society's garden at Wisley, Surrey, the Chelsea Flower Show and other London shows; it will give advice on gardening problems, identify varieties of fruit and send a copy of the Society's monthly journal

---

Boots Garden Chemical Products *

Product	Active Ingredient	Effective against
Herbicides		
Nettle Killer	2,4,5-T	brambles, briars, nettles
Sodium Chlorate	sodium chlorate crystals	deep-rooted weeds, nettles, grasses
Insecticides and Acaricides		
Ant Destroyer	gamma-HCH powder	ants, lice, earwigs
Calomel Dust	mercurous chloride powder	club root, cabbage root fly
Derris Dust	derris powder	general insecticide
Garden Insect Killer	gamma-HCH, pyrethrins and piperonyl	aphids
Garden Insect Powder	carbaryl dust	caterpillars, capsids, earwigs
Greenfly Killer	malathion	aphids
Systemic Greenfly Killer	dimethoate	aphids
Slug Destroyer	metaldehyde pellets	slugs, snails

In addition to the above, Boots also sell their own range of potting compost and seed and cutting compost in large and small bags; a general garden fertiliser in 1- and 3-kg bags; a liquid fertiliser; tomato fertiliser; rose fertilisers and a number of lawn treatments.

*This range of chemicals is in stock at the time of going to press. The full range is available from larger Boots branches.

Index